Resolving Identity-Based Conflict

Jay Rothman

Resolving Identity-Based Conflict

in Nations, Organizations,

and Communities

JOSSEY-BASS
A Wiley Imprint
www.josseybass.com

Published by Jossey-Bass
A Wiley Imprint
989 Market Street, San Francisco, CA 94103-1741   www.josseybass.com

Definition of *resolve* used by permission, from *Merriam-Webster's 3rd New International Dictionary* (Unabridged), 1993 by Merriam-Webster Inc., publisher of the Merriam-Webster dictionaries.

Excerpt from "Onward and Upward with the Arts" by James Traub, from *The New Yorker* Aug/Sept 1996, reprinted with permission.

Readers should be aware that Internet Web sites offered as citations and/or sources for further information may have changed or disappeared between the time this was written and when it is read.

Jossey-Bass books and products are available through most bookstores. To contact Jossey-Bass directly call our Customer Care Department within the U.S. at 800-956-7739, outside the U.S. at 317-572-3986, or fax 317-572-4002.

Jossey-Bass also publishes its books in a variety of electronic formats. Some content that appears in print may not be available in electronic books.

Library of Congress Cataloging-in-Publication Data

Rothman, Jay.
    Resolving identity-based conflict in nations, organizations, and communities / Jay Rothman.
        p. cm. — (The Jossey-Bass conflict resolution series)
    Includes bibliographical references (p.) and index.
    ISBN 0-7879-0996-3 (cloth)
    1. Conflict management. 2. Group identity. 3. Pluralism (Social sciences)
I. Title. II. Series.
HM136.R675 1997
303.6'9—dc21
                                                    97–4719

FIRST EDITION

9 8 7 6 5

The Jossey-Bass Conflict Resolution Series

• •

The Jossey-Bass Conflict Resolution Series addresses the growing need for guidelines in the field of conflict resolution, as broadly defined to include negotiation, mediation, alternative dispute resolution, and other forms of third-party intervention. Our books bridge theory and practice, ranging from descriptive analysis to prescriptive advice. Our goal is to provide those engaged in understanding and finding new and more effective ways to approach conflict—practitioners, researchers, teachers, and those in other professional and volunteer pursuits—with the resources to further their work and better the world in which we live.

This series is dedicated to
the life and work of
Jeffrey Z. Rubin
1941–1995

Contents

Preface

. . . .

Several years ago I helped run a conflict resolution workshop in the Caucasus region of the former Soviet Union, a region with one of the world's highest densities of different, and contending, ethnic groups. About fifteen of these groups were represented at the workshop. Each night the participants would gather for vodka and more relaxed conversation, which often included stories of military brawn and bravado told by a Chechen political functionary named Shamil. One night the vodka was flowing a little more freely than usual, and this 6'5", three-hundred-pound Chechen announced, "Now, I will dance!" The group became still as Shamil began his traditional Chechen dance. Soon he was virtually flying through the air, slapping his huge hands against his knees and feet. The passion of his dance, of his identity, seemed to levitate him off the ground. Six months later when Russian troops stormed into Chechnya expecting a lightning-fast victory, I thought, "Boris Yeltsin would know there is no way this war will end quickly and easily if he had experienced that Chechen dance." The war raged on for more than three years, finally sputtering to an end with tens of thousands of people dead and a barely disguised Russian defeat.

Identity and conflict are passionate forces indeed. They are two of the most engaging features of human life. When they are combined, the result is a combustible mixture that can either destroy or create, depending upon whether and how the mixture is handled.

Identity conflict has the potential to lead to war and destruction; it also has the potential to generate great creativity and positive transformation. In this book I suggest how identity conflict may be guided toward its creative potential. The book is about making music out of deep conflict.

In opera, singers recite long and sometimes tedious narratives of everyday tensions, strife, and conflict. Such narration (the recitative) works its way toward a more passionate expression and culmination in the aria. Such songs of spirit and passion are the intensification of the everyday. So too with conflict. We have many small disputes daily within ourselves and in our relationships; from time to time, more often in some places and times than others, conflicts strike at our core, our identities. Then we become passionate. How can this passion be guided? How can conflict be channeled to enhance group identity and positive intergroup relations rather than provoke antagonism, domination, or even war?

This book defines and addresses identity conflicts that take place within and between national, organizational, and community groups in which individuals invest their hopes for a meaningful, safe, and dignified life. It shows how such conflict, which often brings out the worst in people, can also call forth the best in people.

One of the reasons identity-based conflict is so engaging is that it is so visceral. It comes from—and hits us—in our gut. Our emotions, identities, and bodies are often on the line. Deep conflict requires a tremendous exertion of psychological and physical energy. Although the philosopher William James (1910, p. 3) was on the right track when he called on humanity to wage peace—"the moral equivalent of war," he did not tell us concretely how to do so. As long as we turn to the art of war and violence to address our deep conflicts instead of nurturing the art of peace and cooperation, the former will prevail. Avoiding, yelling, pushing, punching, or even pulling a gun are relatively easy reactions to conflict and may even be initially satisfying for an aggrieved party. Finding ways to foster common cause, to think together and solve problems for mutual benefit, to make peace pay—all take painstaking and heroic effort. A constructive cycle of cooperation may be even more powerful, and certainly more creative, than the unfortunately more common vicious cycle of violence. "Who is a hero?" ask the rabbis of the Talmud. Their answer: "One who changes an enemy into an ally."

Still, conflict resolution is not necessarily a polite process. Transforming deep conflict through creative means toward a peaceful end is not about being nice or making pleasantries with an adversary. Nor is it about forging feelings of fellowship or necessarily enhancing trust. Although these may be results of the peace-making process, they are not its engine. Transforming conflict is about finding that even the bitterest of adversaries share common human needs. Identity conflict is about who we really are and what we care about most deeply. Such conflict may be creatively transformed when adversaries come to learn, ironically perhaps, that they may fulfill their deepest needs and aspirations only with the cooperation of those who most vigorously oppose them. Even while cooperating, adversaries may still wish the other side would just go away; peace prevails when they understand that this will not happen. Through in-depth encounters, even the angriest of enemies may come to learn that just as their own needs for expression and fulfillment of identity, safety, dignity, and meaning are like a thirst that must be quenched, the other side's identity needs are equally compelling.

When we push forward and engage deep conflicts—in our nations, organizations, and communities—music can result. In the process of engagement, our identities, which may be threatened or frustrated by such conflicts, may be refined like gold in a smelting furnace. The dross falls away and burns up as the precious core remains. Although this may sound idealistic or unrealistic, in fact for the past several decades, the emerging field of conflict resolution has seen an evolution of theories and practices for concretely transforming bitter conflicts into opportunities. War is more prevalent than peace, and violent conflict is more common than cooperation, but the battle for peace is on. By writing *Resolving*

Identity-Based Conflict, I seek to contribute my voice to this wealth of theory and experience.

This book results from my own study and practical synthesis of many models of conflict resolution. It began with a journey more than twenty years ago, when I went to Israel for a short visit. Arriving as an assimilated American Jew, with little time or patience for ethnic or cultural exclusivity, I put my head against the Western Wall in the old city of Jerusalem and felt a powerful surge—a rich connection to a people, a religion, a culture, a history. For the first time I knew what it meant to have a passionate connection—an identity that is mine yet is so much larger than I am.

However, I soon began asking, Must this identity be pursued and fulfilled in opposition to that of another people, the Palestinians? Moreover, I wondered how I could reconcile my own universalistic and humanistic side with my newly found, particularistic identity. My answer to both questions came first from books. For months I struggled with *I and Thou* by Martin Buber and found there a "believing humanism" that has guided me since. Next I discovered in the work of the father of cultural pluralism, Horace Kallen, an answer to the question of how to be simultaneously particularistic and universalistic in my identity as a Jew and as a man of the world. By deeply living my own cultural and religious identity, I could gain access to and connection with others living out theirs.

This led me to the teachings of a black Baptist preacher who, by living his identity, changed the world for all people. At the Martin Luther King, Jr. Center for Non-Violent Social Change, I learned from a Catholic nun, Sister Anne Brotherton, about King's work and philosophy of nonviolence. A decade later I returned to Israel, where I founded and for six years ran the Conflict Resolution Program at the Leonard Davis Institute for International Relations at the Hebrew University of Jerusalem.

Even after I returned to the United States, Jerusalem in many ways remained the central metaphor for my work, which has now branched out to include organizational and community conflicts as well as international relations. In Jerusalem two passionate identity groups diametrically opposed to one another are forced to live uneasily together. Can they do it better than they have? Will Jerusalem be a tinderbox for the next world war or a model for living together peacefully in the next millennium?

Conflict begs to be viewed not merely as a problem waiting to be solved but as an opportunity for growth, cooperation, and development waiting to be fulfilled. Toward this end I have built my work upon some of the best ideas of the interlocking fields of conflict management, resolution, and transformation. The theoretical and applied framework I have synthesized, which I call ARIA, is named for the journey through **A**ntagonism, **R**esonance, **I**nvention, and **A**ction. Surfacing *Antagonism* in deep conflict enables disputants to express buried anger and angst. Moving past this common starting point in conflict discourse, which is often its stopping point as well, the next step is to seek *Resonance* by articulating overlapping needs and values that are at stake for the parties in the conflict. Through *Invention*, former adversaries generate creative solutions to fulfill the needs they seek separately but can only get, or at least can only fully get, cooperatively; finally, planning *Action* and a joint agenda carries the process forward.

The first section of this book presents the ARIA framework, beginning with a brief metaphorical description of an identity conflict within a musical ensemble called the ARIA Quartet, which serves to illustrate the framework in practice. In Chapter One, I develop a definition for identity conflict and explain why conventional conflict management theories and methods are ineffective in solving it. The next four chapters explain each phase of the framework in detail, with illustrations of the process in action. Each phase of the ARIA framework is further brought to life through the continuing story of conflict and resolution in the ARIA Quartet.

The second section provides detailed examples of how ARIA can function in nations, organizations, and communities. In Chapter Six

I focus on the Israeli-Palestinian conflict over Jerusalem. In Chapter Seven I describe organizational applications; Chapter Eight is a sort of training guide for practitioners in which I illustrate how ARIA can be applied to community conflicts.

A challenge I face in my work generally, and with this book in particular, is balancing or bridging the different worlds of theory and practice. I seek in the Lewinian action-research tradition to test out my theory in use and to be rigorous and systematic in my practice so that sound theory can emerge from it. Although the link between theory and practice sounds obvious and necessary to many, particularly in a field of conflict studies and intervention, putting them together often creates friction. So applying my own principles, I seek to integrate these worlds of theory and practice when possible, or at least guide them to a more peaceful and synergistic coexistence.

I have sought to make this book as accessible to readers as possible. The text is as jargon-free and the language as direct as I could make it; when I have to use technical language, I explain it fully and simply. Also I have removed most citations and references from the text. Extensive bibliographic notes can be found in a separate section at the end of the book. I included these notes to acknowledge the fact that my work is built on, sometimes in counterdistinction to, the good efforts and ideas of many, many other people; I want to set the work in its appropriate intellectual context and to acknowledge and discuss the work of those whose shoulders I have looked over or stood upon. Readers who are not interested in the academic and theoretical side of this book may quickly skim the Notes section or ignore it altogether.

Haverford, Pennsylvania   Jay Rothman
March 1997

Acknowledgments

. . . .

The list of people and institutions that have made this book possible is very long, since I have been working on it for six years. It was 1991 when the late Jeffrey Rubin, a leader in the world of conflict resolution, urged me, despite my weariness after having written my first book, "to write the next one." I told him I feared it wouldn't make much of a difference in the world but would certainly take a toll on my life. He countered, "You never know." When Jeffrey died in a tragic accident four years later, I vowed to complete this for him. Here it is, Jeffrey. I do hope it makes some difference.

A number of other people helped me to birth this book—not an easy delivery—and I am eternally grateful to them. Cedric Crocker, my editor at Jossey-Bass, held my hand and encouraged me throughout with just the right amount of warm support and convincing pressure. Karen Ivory, my development editor, is in many ways single-handedly responsible for coaxing this book from its previous chaos to what I believe is now a very coherent and reader-friendly volume. My wife and partner, Randi Land Rothman, greatly assisted me with final editing and refinements to help make this book sing. The Jossey-Bass team, especially Noelle Graney, Nathalie Mainland-Smith, and Michael Long, provided masterful assistance in final stages.

Along the way a number of colleagues read and commented on my drafts, and I am grateful to each of them (though, of course, none bear any responsibility for the book's faults or limitations).

Readers included Victor Friedman, Roy Lewicki, Chris Moore, Marc Ross, Jeffrey Rubin, and Jerry Weissman. My childhood buddy, musician, writer, and illustrator extraordinaire, Tom Bachtell, provided me with a story of conflict in a musical ensemble that I have adapted for this book. He gave this gift to me just as the book was gaining steam, providing it with added zest. It is important to note here that although this book contains many tales of conflict that are based in reality, most drawn from my own practice, they have all been fictionalized and all actors' names and characteristics have been altered.

Over the past decade I have been blessed with wonderful students in many different settings. I have taught at the Hebrew University in Jerusalem; I currently teach at Bryn Mawr and Haverford Colleges, and I have run numerous seminars and workshops at universities and colleges throughout the United States and for disputing parties from different "hot spots" around the world: Cyprus, South Africa, Northern Ireland, Sri Lanka, the former Soviet Union, and elsewhere. As a consultant I have worked with top executives and cafeteria workers, superintendents and school board members, politicians and community organizers. All have been my teachers as well as good students. I am grateful to them all for directly contributing to my work with their comments, criticisms, enthusiasm, and valuable feedback.

The writing of this book began while I was at the Leonard Davis Institute for International Relations running the Project on Prenegotiation, funded by the MacArthur Foundation and the U.S. Institute for Peace. My work there was continued with funding from the Konrad Adenauer Foundation to direct the Program on Managing Political Disputes. Upon returning to the United States, I turned my attention to organizational conflict and am currently supported in an ongoing project that examines the role of conflict in promoting organizational learning. The project is funded by the Daimler-Benz Foundation. I am also engaged in a multiyear project, funded by the Pew Charitable Trusts, to define, promote, and assess success in ethnic conflict resolution. I am grateful to these foundations for their financial support, though it should be noted that the views expressed in the book are mine and not necessarily those of the foundations. Finally, I am grateful to Haverford and Bryn Mawr Colleges for granting me an academic leave, which ultimately made the completion of this project possible.

J. R.

Resolve—"to make (as one or more voice parts
or the total musical harmony) progress
from a dissonance into a consonance."
—Webster's 3rd New
International Dictionary

To my family, for helping me weave my life into a consonance.

About the Author

Jay Rothman is director of The ARIA Group, Inc., a conflict resolution training and consulting firm. He is also scholar-in-residence at the McGregor School of Antioch University in Yellow Springs, Ohio, where he teaches conflict resolution and management seminars. He has worked with diplomats, business executives, opposing leaders of embattled ethnic communities, union leaders, school boards and superintendents, community activists and organizers, and students from around the world. He has been a teacher, trainer, and student of the art and science of conflict resolution: transforming normally destructive and deeply rooted conflicts into opportunities for learning and cooperative action.

Rothman is the author of *From Confrontation to Cooperation: Resolving Ethnic and Regional Conflict,* a study of international conflict resolution (Sage, 1992). It presents his work beginning in 1987 when, as founding director of the Conflict Resolution Program at the Leonard Davis Institute for International Relations at the Hebrew University of Jerusalem, he began his career facilitating conflict resolution workshops between Israelis and Palestinians, Greek and Turkish Cypriots, and loyalist and nationalist leaders from Northern Ireland. During this period he also taught diplomats from a dozen countries, and during the transitional period in South Africa he worked with African National Congress leaders to prepare them for service at the new South African Foreign Ministry.

Over the past several years, with support from the Pew Charitable Trusts, Rothman has been conducting an action-research project to promote and articulate criteria for success in ethnic and community conflict resolution interventions in the United States and around the world. To this end he has developed a systematic "action-evaluation" methodology for community development and conflict resolution.

He has also been a member of a study group project on organizational learning sponsored by the Daimler-Benz Foundation. His contribution to the group's handbook on organizational learning is an essay on the role of conflict in transforming organizational obstacles into opportunities for learning, growth, and sustained change.

A graduate of Antioch College (1980), Rothman received his master of arts (1986) and doctorate (1988) in international relations from the University of Maryland. He also studied conflict resolution at George Mason University and small group dynamics at the National Training Laboratories. His work in conflict resolution began with an internship at the Martin Luther King Jr. Center for Non-Violent Social Change in Atlanta.

Rothman currently lives with his wife and three children in Yellow Springs, Ohio.

◆ ◆ ◆ ◆ ◆ ◆ ◆

For information on a training course based on the ideas presented in this book, visit the author's web site at http://www.ariagroup.com.

Resolving Identity-
Based Conflict

. . . .

Prologue

· ·

The ARIA Quartet Conflict

The ARIA Quartet consists of four outstanding musicians who have performed professionally for many years. During the past year, the group has formed to play together with an eye toward concertizing.

The chemistry was quite good at the beginning, as the group members were simply content to be playing with fellow master musicians. The first symptoms of identity conflict arise around a specific Brahms quartet the group has chosen to prepare for an upcoming performance. "I know we have a chance to give a great concert," Arthur, the first violinist, says to the others. "But as we have prepared for it, I realized we have totally different approaches to the piece, different approaches to performing, actually." Strong-willed and flashy, Arthur strikes some people as antagonistic and boastful. He views the musical score as a single entity with which to become familiar before practicing and perfecting his lead parts on his own. The cellist, Rachel, focuses on the overall resonance and musical quality of the ensemble. She and Anthony, the violist, want the group to spend more time together working on the music section by section, incorporating tempo changes and emotional interpretations from the start. Rachel is dynamic but generally soft-spoken; however, she can be volatile when provoked. Anthony is generally an amiable and optimistic fellow, but he is beginning to feel a bit resentful, even jealous, of Arthur. He and Rachel agree that the different styles in the quartet are quite apparent. "But we are still enjoying making music, and I think if we just keep going, things will work themselves out," Anthony says.

What happens instead is that their enthusiasm starts to fade. The excitement and passion the group had felt for their collaboration turns to frustration and dissatisfaction. "It seems like all of a sudden the lines are drawn," Arthur confides to Isabel, the second violinist. "Rachel and Anthony seem to think we just want to barrel through, and I feel like they are prematurely focusing on subtle interpretations instead of first gaining an overall sense of the piece." Isabel believes both sides are overcompensating during rehearsals, trying to wield some control. "They are making us seasick with their stops and starts, and we are driving them crazy with what they see as our relentless beat and rush to the end." They decide to seek the advice of a music coach at a nearby conservatory.

Part I

· ·

Transforming Identity-Based Conflict

· ·

The ARIA Framework

Antagonism, Resonance, Invention, Action

S ome conflicts just will not go away. The Israelis and the Palestinians have battled each other violently for decades, each side
claiming a right to the same land. Management and labor unions
fight down to the wire on a regular basis, ostensibly over benefits
and wage increases. White and African American communities
grow increasingly isolated from and hostile to one another.

Except for their intransigence these conflicts appear to have little in common, but in significant ways their roots may be quite similar. In each case and in numerous other seriously protracted
national, organizational, and communal conflicts, what often is truly
at stake is overlooked and difficult to identify. At stake in all of
these cases are the primary group identity needs of the disputants.[1]
When people's essential identities, as expressed and maintained by
their primary group affiliations, are threatened or frustrated, intransigent conflict almost inevitably follows. However, in such conflicts,
conventional methods of conflict management are usually inadequate and may even exacerbate the problem. I believe we need a
new approach to analyzing and addressing the growing class of deep
conflicts infused with identity concerns.

The Importance of Identity

Conflicts of all kinds—conflicts between Greeks and Turks in
Cyprus, between various sectors in organizations, between lay and

professional leaders in communities, and even between musicians in an ensemble—have the potential to promote dynamism and creative development. All too often, however, particularly when conflicts are deep, that potential is lost because the conflicts are misdiagnosed and handled poorly. Frequently the result is stagnation, frustration, even violence. Identity conflicts are often hard to identify, since they are usually misrepresented as disputes over tangible resources. Moreover, they often wax and wane, fluctuating in intensity. Sometimes such conflicts are severe; sometimes they go underground. But unless accurately identified and addressed, identity conflicts fester or emerge later with renewed vigor (Azar, 1986).

These conflicts have high stakes for all parties involved. Their intensity often is destructive, as each side seeks to avoid or subdue the other. Collective identity conflicts are usually intransigent and resistant to resolution. They are deeply rooted in the underlying individual human needs and values that together constitute people's social identities, particularly in the context of group affiliations, loyalties, and solidarity. Such intransigence is clearly evident in ethnic conflicts, which serve as a prototype for identity conflict in this book. Although ethnic conflicts are the most intense identity conflicts, they are certainly not the only cases in which we find collective identity to be at the core. Similar roots and existential concerns can be apparent in the needs and frustrations, the hopes and fears, of groups at almost any level of society. While people may believe, for example, that their protracted organizational conflict has nothing in common with a long-standing international crisis, once the underlying issues are articulated, they may come to realize that many of the essential identity concerns are similar.[2]

Ethnic groups around the world, feeling reviled and disregarded by majority groups holding power, react by militating for independent statehood or at least autonomy. Soon the struggle for political expression, as it is resisted, becomes the group's main cause; their underlying motives—the identity threats and frustrations—become obscured. Intransigent conflicts in parts of Africa, Northern Ireland,

Cyprus, the Balkans, Sri Lanka, the Middle East, and dozens of other trouble spots around the globe are characterized by long-standing, seemingly insoluble tensions. While they may well be manifested in conventional ways, such as rivalries over territory or competition for scarce resources, these conflicts are often more deeply rooted in existential issues like cultural expression and survival itself.[3]

Many labor-management conflicts, often apparently fought over resources like wages and benefits, surface again and again even after compromises and settlements are reached. Frequently these resource disputes mask deeper identity concerns that are not addressed, such as control, participation, and efficacy.[4] Community groups holding very strong views about moral issues, such as abortion or affirmative action, perpetually clash over contradictory priorities and values. In short, identities are in conflict, although these are rarely explored analytically through rational dialogue. Instead they get caught up in acrimonious debates and battles over legislation and influence.

Identity-driven conflicts are rooted in the articulation of, and the threats or frustrations to, people's collective need for dignity, recognition, safety, control, purpose, and efficacy. Unfortunately, they are all too rarely framed in that way. The hypothesis that runs throughout this book is that group identity conflicts are an increasingly important and identifiable class of conflict, with patterns and characteristics that run within and among all levels of social organization, both domestic and international. These conflicts are often destructive, but with the right analysis and approach they may become enormously creative and transformative. All conflicts, but intense group identity conflicts in particular, provide significant opportunities for dynamism and growth.

For growth to occur, conflicts must be effectively managed, resolved, transformed, or engaged.[5] Conflict engagement is what takes place between the extremes of avoidance or confrontation (Figure 1.1); it can lead to dynamism, creativity, and growth. In my work generally and in this book in particular, my goal is to help analysts, adversaries, and third parties identify identity conflicts and engage them proactively.[6]

Breaking the Pattern

Creative engagement in deep and persistent identity-driven conflict begins when all sides can give voice to their essential concerns and can hear and recognize the essential concerns of the other side as well. Indeed, the potential for voice and recognition in identity conflicts is what makes them so promising. Although not often done, it is both possible and necessary for disputants in bitter and protracted identity conflicts to engage in constructive dialogue about the nature of their conflict. Such dialogue can build a foundation for reconciliation and joint action. That is the end benefit of a dialogue process in which parties fully express and understand the deep concerns that drive their conflicts, both in their own specific context or group and from the perspective of their opponents. Where before there was a stalemate, now there is movement.

To creatively manage a conflict when individual and group identity is at stake, core concerns—survival, recognition, dignity—must be surfaced and addressed. When conflict is rooted in the protection of identity needs, the stakes are far greater than in interest-based conflict born out of competition over resources. In identity

Figure 1.1. Conflict Engagement: Between Avoidance and Confrontation

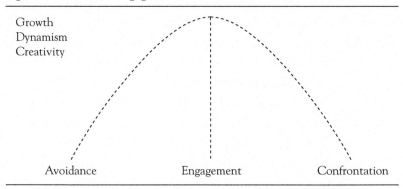

Growth
Dynamism
Creativity

Avoidance   Engagement   Confrontation

conflict, groups struggle for their basic physical and moral survival. Accordingly, the potential for destruction or creativity is strong.

We must differentiate identity-based conflicts from those rooted primarily in interests, because the conventional approaches to handling interest-based disputes often serve only to exacerbate identity conflicts. Traditional approaches to negotiation and conflict management focus essentially on interests—the very tangible, practical resources over which people often compete. The Western culture of negotiation has developed on that foundation, with the law being the most prototypical mechanism for dealing with interest-based conflicts. We legislate, adjudicate, and compromise.

However, with identity conflicts, both legal mechanisms and conventional negotiation approaches can simply add fuel to the fire. Compromise in particular is commonly viewed as a primary goal of negotiation or problem solving. In identity conflicts, trying to compromise at the outset may be counter-productive, or impossible, because what is at stake are people's existential needs and values. Compromising over such essential concerns as safety, dignity, control over destiny, or ultimately over identity, is out of the question. These things are not up for bargaining. If people feel they will be forced to compromise over such existential issues, they dig in their heels and say, "No way! I'd much rather have this conflict." The cost of compromise is not worth the benefit of settlement.

What is necessary instead is a dialogue that leads to a surfacing and practical reconciliation of needs and values. Such dialogue fosters a rich articulation and recognition of the roots of a conflict. Through a guided discussion about what adversaries care about most deeply and why, disputants may begin to speak so their opponents can listen, and listen so their opponents can speak. Such dialogue makes possible reconciliatory action to transform destructive tendencies into creative realities.

In this chapter I will define identity conflicts and show how they differ from resource-based conflicts. I will discuss why traditional methods of negotiation and some more recent approaches to conflict management are often ineffective with identity conflicts. Finally, I will introduce a framework called ARIA as one effective approach to fostering dialogue and cooperative action in identity conflicts.

Distinguishing Identity Conflicts

In seeking to define what makes identity conflict a specific and important class of conflict, it is useful to contrast it with more every-day and routine forms of disputes. Many conflicts contain elements that are relatively obvious, observable, and tangible. A landlord and tenant struggle over value, that is, the tenant wants more services, for which the landlord wants more rent. Several nations compete for a single economic market. A potential employee demands a higher salary offer before agreeing to accept a job. These may be referred to, in short, as resource-based or interest-based conflicts.

Interest-based disputes are usually concrete and clearly defined, and the outcomes each side seeks are bounded by the resources at stake: more or less land, wages and benefits, or military and economic power. The usefulness of cooperative outcomes or mutual accommodation in such disputes is often not too difficult to discern, and thus negotiation and problem solving are relatively easy to initiate and sustain. For example, high-level negotiations were held for many years at the United Nations to determine the "Law of the Sea." Nations bordering oceans, and those land-locked, sought to reach common ground on exploiting and protecting the seas' resources. Fisher and Ury (1981) describe a conflict between the United States and India when the latter proposed an initial fee for companies mining the seas of $60 million per site (p. 87). The United States rejected this entirely. Both sides dug in. Eventually focusing on shared interests—that the seas be equitably used and shared by rich and poor nations alike—they found a way to set a fee that was not exorbitant and prohibitive but one that would still ensure that rich countries and companies would pay for the use of the seas such that poorer countries would also benefit. This was an interest-based conflict, and negotiation techniques were used effectively to ameliorate it.

However, many other conflicts are relatively intangible and deeply rooted in the more abstract and interpretive dynamics of history, psychology, culture, values, and beliefs of identity groups. Israelis and Palestinians battle over issues of safety and control. Labor and management battle over issues of organizational survival and participation. Communities battle over issues of tradition versus change. These are identity conflicts because they derive from existential and underlying psychocultural concerns that are perceived as threatened or frustrated as a result of, or resulting in, intransigent conflict.[7] These disputes are usually, at their source, very complex, relatively intangible, and often hard to define clearly. However, they regularly become simplified and focused upon scarce resources which, though concrete, overshadow or even subvert the deeper elements at stake.

Rooted as they are in complex and multidimensional psychological, historical, and cultural factors, identity conflicts are marked by a difficulty in clear determination of their parameters and boundaries. In fact such conflicts are so intangible and hard to define because they arise from the depths of the human heart rather than the material world. Although theoretical distinctions between identity and interest conflicts may be valid, the differences are not so neat or clear-cut in practice. It is fair to say that all identity conflicts contain interest conflicts; not all interest conflicts contain identity conflicts. Many do, however, particularly the longer they go on. What is most crucial at the outset of a conflict engagement process is to analyze the depth and type of a conflict at a given time, then to ascertain how it should be treated. It can be difficult to discover the salience of the issues at stake. Is the conflict based mostly in resources or identity issues? The challenge is to know which level should be addressed, and when. Conflicts that start primarily as interest-based, when ignored or poorly handled may evolve into identity conflicts; the longer a conflict continues, the more people connect their dignity and prestige with the dispute. Conversely, identity conflicts addressed as if they were primarily about resources may grow from bad to worse. Given the natural human disposition for the concrete and measurable, identity conflicts often are misidentified as resource-based disputes and approached inappropriately.

The Problem with Conventional Negotiation Techniques

Identity conflicts require that special efforts be made to ensure accurate analysis, definition, and amelioration precisely because such conflicts are not tangible. Common modes of bargaining in which disputants converge on mutually acceptable concessions are often useful in well-defined, tangible, resource-based conflicts. However, they can have disastrous effects when conflicts are poorly defined and intangible. Moreover, an attempt to separate people's basic concerns from their substantive problems, as commonly prescribed for effective negotiation behavior, is impossible when the core issue is identity itself. Any effort to do so may lead to an obfuscation and to further frustration of the essential issues at stake.

It is possible to fully analyze a conflict at an early stage, but it takes time. An initial investment of time and energy, or going slow to go fast, does have its payoffs. This could be seen as the *long-short way*. Spending a substantial amount of time up front analyzing and defining a problem can considerably shorten the time required to work out a solution that lasts (Figure 1.2).

If the conflict is fully and clearly defined at the beginning of a conflict engagement process, then the search for solutions is likely to be efficient. Early conflict definition will also help determine which type of conflict processing techniques will be most effective.

Although negotiation is often a cooperative and integrative process, it is most commonly viewed as a process designed to get all sides to split their differences, to compromise, to converge on concessions. Compromise in this form of negotiation is most successful when the goals are well defined and when there is an accepted com-

Figure 1.2. Going Slow to Go Fast.

The "Short-Long" Way (short-cutting definitions, leading to inefficient and ineffective solutions)

Problem Definition   ------>   S o l u t i o n   S e e k i n g

---

The "Long-Short" Way (taking time with definitions, leading to effective and efficient solutions)

P r o b l e m   D e f i n i t i o n   ------>   Solution Seeking

---

mon ground. This, by definition, is not the case in most identity conflicts, when the underlying issues are blurred and the stakes—like moral or physical survival—are very high. Thus these conflicts protract and deepen. While conventional negotiating techniques, like early solution seeking, are quite effective in some circumstances, they are frequently misapplied when core issues have not yet been clearly defined. If the time has not been spent to analyze what a conflict is truly about, then negotiation may be rushed and counter-productive, serving to exacerbate and deepen hostilities.

Negotiation and bargaining too early in a conflict engagement process can make identity conflicts worse. If the parties are forced toward a compromise that they will later regret, they may be driven further apart in the end. It is difficult enough for conflicting parties to sit down together, but if the sessions are fruitless, or if they result in intensified anger, then it will be even harder to conduct sessions in the future. Premature negotiation or problem solving, particularly in identity conflicts, can result in severe setbacks to the process of peace making.

Just as it is essential to determine when disputants are locked in an identity conflict, so it is necessary to change the thinking about how such adversaries should interact if true peace is sought. In adversarial bargaining, the cards are held tightly to the chest; parties posture about what they really want, knowing they will have to compromise on their opening positions. As one of the masters of this type of negotiation, Henry Kissinger (1961) writes, "If agreement is usually found between two starting points, there is no point in making moderate offers. Good bargaining techniques would suggest a point of departure far more extreme than what one is willing to accept. The more outrageous the initial proposition, the better is the prospect that what one *really* wants will be considered a compromise" (p. 205). The somewhat counter-intuitive, and certainly counter-experiential, suggestion here is that a way must be found to enable parties locked in deep identity conflicts to show their cards and articulate what is really at stake, what they really care about most deeply, and why. If they do not, negotiations and other forms of conflict management, if and when they eventually occur, will not succeed in addressing underlying concerns. Opponents need to know more, not less, about each other's intentions, motivations, and objectives. Unfortunately, this is precisely the kind of information opponents often seek to hide from one another, believing that in this way they may best keep their options open or manipulate the other side.

The art of negotiation has been classically viewed as one of deceit and subterfuge. As Francois de Callieres suggested in describing negotiation during the reign of Louis XIV in the early eighteenth century, the more one could discover the true intentions and feelings of one's opponents, the better one could manipulate them during negotiation. In such a situation the best offense was a good defense, and the great negotiator was he who could "make himself absolute master of all the outward effects which passion usually produced, so much so that neither in his speech nor by the least change in his countenance could one discover his real thought . . . " (de Callieres, 1963).

This type of bargaining may be effective in the game of convergence and concession but only when the goals are well defined and when there is an accepted common ground. For instance, the bargaining between an employer and employee contains clear guidelines for how the negotiation will proceed. The goal is clear—

a wage offer that is satisfactory to both. And there is a common ground, since both parties want to find an acceptable wage rate so that employment can proceed. There is, prior to the negotiation, a tacit agreement that it is in the best interests of each party to find a satisfactory solution. Parties in such situations recognize their interdependence, accept that there are preferable alternatives to the conflict, are confident they can reach agreement with the other side, and view negotiation as the means to that end.

In identity conflicts it may well be a fatal mistake to try to find areas for concession and convergence before the conflicting parties can see the advantage of reaching a negotiated settlement. However, once identity conflicts are under control, with disputants working together to find a solution that will fulfill underlying needs and concerns of both sides, conventional negotiation or interest-based bargaining is appropriate. What is needed first is an analytical and *wholly* cooperative approach that sets the stage for the problem solving and the "mixed-motive" negotiation (both cooperative and competitive) that will come later. The ARIA framework is designed to address cases in which normal negotiation is premature; the ARIA process serves to ripen the situation so the groundwork is laid for successful conflict management.

When the stakes are high—for safety, dignity, identity—compromise, even over symbolic issues, can be viewed as existentially threatening. Therefore, an interactive dialogue must precede problem solving or negotiating, and should accomplish several important goals: the parties must learn to appreciate the gains of reaching an agreement; they must begin to look at their conflict in common terms, articulating shared concerns and aspirations; all sides must appreciate the advantage of reaching an agreement that the others find fair and acceptable; and finally, the parties must feel comfortable with the climate for negotiations that will result in mutual gains. In short the essential goals and motivations of all parties locked in identity conflict must be fully articulated and at least accepted in principle prior to problem solving.

That is not an easy feat. As noted earlier, our culture of negotiation teaches us to be secretive, manipulative, and somewhat devious. But such approaches are especially counter-productive in identity-based conflict. They often lead to competitive bargaining over the wrong issues at the wrong time, with the wrong people. Such bargaining will likely lead to further conflict intransigence. For instance, bargaining over territory or wage and benefit packages when the real conflicts are about dignity, safety, or participation will ultimately decrease the chances of successful negotiation procedures or outcomes.

One negative legacy of the subterfuge model of negotiation is that it provides a disincentive to engage in joint inquiry and cooperative conflict analysis. The ultimate effectiveness of conflict management, and parties' willingness to risk engaging in it, "depends in large part upon the exchange of sufficient credible information between parties" (Rubin and Brown, 1975, p. 52). However, in most conflict such communication is limited. In situations of intransigent conflict, it is severely circumscribed.

The ARIA framework is designed to address the problem of inadequate and inaccurate information exchange between disputants by contributing to the evolution of openness and an atmosphere of joint inquiry and learning. To launch successful negotiation or problem solving in identity conflicts, the groundwork must first be laid by enabling disputants to give voice to their deepest concerns and essential motivations, and to recognize those of their adversaries.

Too often identity conflicts are interpreted as resource conflicts and incorrectly addressed, and thereby are deepened and prolonged (Exhibit 1.1). For example, for decades the Arab-Israeli conflict was defined and sustained in resource terms as a struggle between two nations over one piece of real estate. Efforts to redefine the conflict in terms of its human dimensions and break the barriers of fear, insecurity, and mutual nonrecognition began at unofficial levels that later were consolidated in formal agreements. The shape of an eventual solution began to emerge in the early 1990s when the conflict was politically reframed in terms of the underlying human needs and values at

Exhibit 1.1. Identity-Based versus Resource-Based Conflicts.

Identity Conflict	Resource-Based Conflict
Source	
Needs and Values	*Resources*
Threats to or frustration over such identity needs as dignity, safety, control	Competition over material and territorial interests
Characteristics	
Intangible	*Tangible*
Rooted in history, psychology, culture, belief systems	Focused on finite goods or services: Socioeconomic factors,
Abstract and complex goals	resource scarcity. Concrete, with goals clearly defined
Initial Engagement	
Interactive	*Transactive*
Dialogue about needs and values promoting voice and recognition	Interest-based and mixed-motive bargaining

stake for Israelis and Palestinians. As Palestinian leadership began formally recognizing Israel's right to security and sovereignty, many Israelis began to show a willingness to negotiate compromises over territory. Similarly, when many Israelis began recognizing Palestinian national aspirations as legitimate, growing numbers of Palestinians became willing to accept only part of Palestine as their state.

When the sources of insecurity that mark identity conflicts are brought to the surface and needs are addressed—at least in principle—some of the deepest conflicts begin to become negotiable. The ARIA process can help bring about this change.

The ARIA Framework

True music is born of understanding. Technical mastery is necessary, but clarity of interpretation and motivation are even more critical.

Inspired by music, the ARIA method begins with those same assumptions; in addition, conflict within the ARIA framework is viewed as a potential source of great creativity.

Only when people are clear about their own values and motivations can they truly say what they mean. And only when they can fully articulate what they mean can they act upon their ideas. Conflict arises from a mismatch of words and deeds, which is itself rooted in lack of clarity. It is not that people intentionally deceive themselves or lack integrity when engaged in conflict; rather, their own tacit assumptions usually remain just that—tacit, unarticulated, and unexamined. Deep conflict, if it is to be transformed and made creative, requires a profound clarity of thought and action; forging an integration of thought and action is one of the gifts of successful conflict engagement and may be profoundly transforming.

I refer to the dialogue and reconciliation process that seeks this integration of words and deeds as the *ARIA framework* (Figure 1.3). The ultimate goal of the ARIA framework is to foster harmony and resonance from adversaries' full and honest expression of the deeply felt human motivations that lie beneath their conflict. Through a process of staged adversarial framing, when the focus is on the *what* of the conflict—what resources are at stake and what solutions are being sought—antagonism is surfaced. An underlying sense of resonance is then fostered through reflexive reframing, when the questions are now *who* (not as categories but as persons) and *why*, and the core identity issues are articulated. This sets the stage for inventing joint solutions—the *how*—and finally agenda setting, that is, consolidating the *what, why, who,* and *how* of the previous steps and sustaining them through joint action. In sum, the ARIA framework fosters the articulation and development of four unfolding outcomes: **A**ntagonism, **R**esonance, **I**nvention, and **A**ction.

Although the model is presented here in cyclical form for ease of conceptualization, it is in fact a much more dynamic process when applied. Each phase often leads back to earlier phases, which can influence how later phases are addressed.

Figure 1.3. The ARIA Framework.

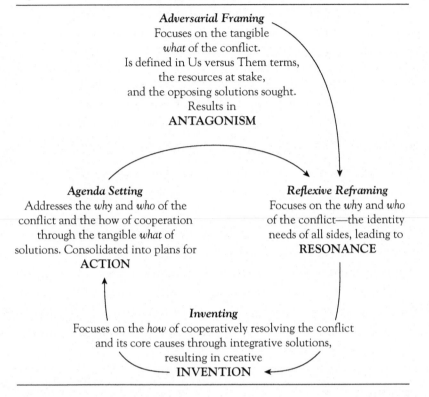

Adversarial Framing
Focuses on the tangible
what of the conflict.
Is defined in Us versus Them terms,
the resources at stake,
and the opposing solutions sought.
Results in
ANTAGONISM

Agenda Setting
Addresses the *why* and *who* of the
conflict and the how of cooperation
through the tangible *what* of
solutions. Consolidated into plans for
ACTION

Reflexive Reframing
Focuses on the *why* and *who*
of the conflict—the identity
needs of all sides, leading to
RESONANCE

Inventing
Focuses on the *how* of cooperatively resolving the conflict
and its core causes through integrative solutions,
resulting in creative
INVENTION

Each step of the ARIA method will be discussed in detail in the following chapters. A brief guide to the process is as follows:

- Antagonism surfaces the battle. It brings out festering angst and anger and puts them out for discussion. It is also useful later in providing a negative frame of reference such as, "We don't want to do that anymore!"

- Resonance fosters a harmony that can emerge between disputants, a harmony growing out of a deep exploration and articulation of what goes on within them. It grows from an expression of the needs and values that have been threatened or frustrated by the conflict and the relations between adversaries. They may discover that "We are in this together."

- Inventing is the process of brainstorming mutually acceptable, creative, and integrative options for addressing central and underlying aspects of the conflict. They learn that "We can get out of this together."

- Action is then built upon the previous stages, implementing what should be done and why, by whom, and how.

Once intransigent identity conflicts are addressed in this way, conventional problem solving and negotiation toward forging and implementing concrete agreements may become possible. When the groundwork is laid and there is an awareness of overlapping motivations and goals, adversaries can fully appreciate the possibilities of cooperating to achieve those goals.

Just as conflict can bring out the worst in people, so it can bring out the best. We have seen the worst in the last decade, as we have witnessed horrendous conflicts around the globe from Rwanda and Bosnia to the Middle East and beyond. Unfortunately, the list is long. But conflict can also call out what is good in people and their communities, organizations, and nations. It can bring out the most profound feelings that people have about what gives their lives meaning. Identity conflict is promising because it contains and brings to light people's core needs and values. Through a process of interactive introspection, such conflict can even bring people closer to those they have hated and fought for centuries—not necessarily as friends, but as partners in the process of articulating and fulfilling their respective identity needs and values. As people on one side of a conflict begin to find their own voices and sing their own songs, those on the other side can learn to listen and to make their own music as well. Resonance results.

2

Antagonism

Surfacing Differences and Analyzing Animosity

Framing focuses attention. When a frame is put around a painting, it gives the viewer a focus. Conflict framing does the same thing. It concentrates attention; it provides a focus on what is at stake in a conflict. Before any attempt at conflict management begins, those involved, whether as adversaries or negotiators, naturally go through a process of conflict framing.[1] The most common way to frame a conflict is to assert the exclusive outcomes disputants seek, that is, to ask, *Who wants what?* To launch a constructive process of conflict engagement, such implicit and generally unhelpful conflict frames must be made explicit and thus available for scrutiny, evaluation, and reframing. Bringing antagonism to the surface is the intended end result of an adversarial framing process that is often automatic and usually unexamined.

An effective way to get disputants to articulate their normal conflict frames is to elicit their positions about their definition and their favored outcomes by asking simply, What is the problem? Either interactively in a workshop format, or in a separate interview with each side, disputants will regularly frame the problem in competitive terms that focus on the tangible, often resource-based outcomes they seek. Within their definition of the problem, each side will normally propose solutions that it feels best enhance its competitive edge. For example, parties in dispute about territory might say, "Their aggression is the problem, and getting back the land they stole from us is the solution."

The fatal flaw with the normal adversarial approach is that it often leads parties to struggle unsuccessfully to resolve their respective and exclusive solutions instead of really focusing first on the nature of their problem. When disputants become polarized, what matters most to them is often lost in the jockeying to better position their side, to score points, to win arguments. They may come to forget their original concerns as the battle becomes its own reward. The first phase in the ARIA framework seeks to show that such "victories" are often false and are followed by renewed and more entrenched conflict.

Intervention must often work backward before it can go forward. Surfacing antagonism is viewed as a necessary, if unpleasant, starting point in the ARIA framework. It begins somewhat counterintuitively by staging an argument. This phase is designed to make explicit what was implicit, to make apparent and thus available for analysis and decision making what was tacit and hidden. This chapter is about this first phase of ARIA: adversarial framing leading to a surfacing of antagonism. The ARIA Quartet conflict, which is further described at the end of this chapter, will provide an illustration of how antagonism may be fruitfully surfaced.

Positions: Who Wants What?

Adversaries locked in serious conflicts often see the world in black and white. They know what they want, and that outcome is usually the opposite of what their opponents want. The mutually exclusive positions of each side can be formed in response to the question, Who wants what? These positions summarize a party's definition of the problem and their solution (in a best-case scenario short of war or aggression) in the form of some kind of compromise or distribution of resources. It is not that this frame is wrong; resources certainly are, or come to be, at stake as parties confront each other. However, by focusing on tangible outcomes of a conflict rather than on the conflict's evolution and underlying causes, adversaries are unable to look first and fully at what is so important to them in the conflict. This tunnel vision precludes a critical exploration of alternative outcomes or, equally important, whether different frames and definitions might better articulate the root causes of the conflict.

Moreover, how parties view the other side greatly influences their approach. If the other side is simply a competitor over scarce resources, then compromise and a fair distribution may be a sufficient settlement. However, if the other side is perceived as a dangerous adversary threatening or frustrating identity needs, the common starting place is to draw a line in the sand between Us and Them. Each side feels relatively blameless, and each sees the opponents as aggressive, perhaps even evil. Abraham Maslow said, "One can spend a lifetime assigning blame, finding causes 'out there' for all troubles that exist" (1972, p. 86). It follows that if a conflict is framed antagonistically, solutions will be sought accordingly; adversarial conflict processing makes creative and cooperative change impossible.

Still, surfacing antagonism does serve several important purposes: it allows a period of emotional venting that can bring buried and pent-up issues to the surface; it presents a point of comparison and contrast to the process that will follow; and it helps create motivation for change. If the antagonism is painful and frustrating, as it almost always is, disputants may develop the determination to try something different. Part of the gain in ARIA comes from the pain of antagonism. When I work with disputants locked in deep conflict, I frequently suggest that creative solutions and cooperative frameworks are there waiting to be mined. However, the process we begin with usually regresses to unproductive haggling and blaming before it can move forward into something new and mutually satisfying. "How do you feel?" I often ask at the end of this phase, and "How shall we proceed?" The response is usually "Awful" and then, "Not like this!"

The Fuel of Antagonism

Adversarial framing, particularly of identity-based conflicts, consists of at least four key processes:

- *Blaming* the other side for the conflict

- *Polarizing* our side against theirs

- *Attributing* negative character and disposition to the opponents

- *Projecting* unacceptable traits from one's own side onto another side

The result of sticking to adversarial framing is invariably conflict escalation, and the positive potential of conflict—for dynamism, creativity, and change—is buried.

Blaming. Blame is the first step in an escalating cycle of conflict.

The most common reaction to conflict is to blame the other side, to draw clear lines between Us and Them, to clear our conscience from aggression while locating its source as wholly external. Blaming is a simple thing to do; in conflict, it is the very simplest thing to do. Children are masters of blaming. A child accused of hitting will say, "He hit me first!" But not only children blame the other side quickly, fully, and without reflection. The tactic is also commonplace among adults and the groups they form and sustain. By blaming "mean-spirited" management, workers believe they absolve themselves of responsibility. By focusing on the foes of affirmative action, supporters assure themselves of their moral superiority. By blaming the Israelis for their oppression, Palestinians can demand that the Arab world support their liberation struggle. By blaming Arabs for their difficulties in nation building, Israelis can externalize their own polarizing internal divisions and forge a working unity around an external adversary.

Blaming others enables us to view the source of conflict as external. "It's those jerks who are causing all the problems—get rid of them and everything will be better." One functional outcome of this kind of blaming is that parties can define themselves as distinct from one another.

In complex systems, particularly when fundamental values are at stake, rarely if ever does isolated blame accurately frame a conflict in full and useful ways. Rather it blurs all distinctions among opponents. They generalize about each other, saying, for example, "They're all that way," thus reducing the complexity of the dispute and making it all but impossible to discover common ground. What regularly happens instead is that the underlying and motivating issues fester. Attempted solutions addressing the symptoms are temporary, often leading to an exacerbation of negative conflict dynamics and antagonism.

Polarizing. An Us-against-Them mentality is required for perpetuating blame; it is also self-fulfilling.

Accepting that one's side may be partly responsible for a conflict is usually painful. Thus ways to avoid such an admission are often found. Instead, the conflict is viewed as rooted in the injurious, wrongful, malicious behavior of Them.

For example, at a board meeting, a school superintendent exclaims that he is fed up with the attacks on him from the community. He asserts that he is being further undermined by a lack of support from board members sitting around the table. Several board members retort that they are also being attacked by the community and are continuously undermined by the superintendent's actions. Furthermore, they assert that they do defend him but are never acknowledged for it. Instead of analyzing their own role in the conflict escalation, each party circles its wagons and views the other as the front line in a two-tiered attack. Neither stops to inquire into the other's insecurity and injury, hope or fear, nor to ask about support the other side had actually offered. Both assume an Us-against-Them situation, thereby further making it so.

Attributing. Negative attribution is unequivocal: everything bad
they do against us is innate to their disposition and character;
everything we do against them is justified as a reaction to a particular situation.

One very common way for parties to perpetuate blame is to
attribute the aggressive actions of their adversaries to a fundamental aspect of their character. The other side is viewed as innately
hostile, aggressive, perhaps even evil. Conversely, the aggression of
one's own side is viewed as a necessary and justified reaction to the
difficult situation, most likely viewed as caused by the evil other.
Trust is impossible and blame is further justified. Based on such an
attributional bias, adversaries regularly believe that their essential
concerns are threatened precisely because there is something
innately aggressive about their adversaries.[2]

The most obvious feature of such attributions is that they are
reductionist. They rely on a selective perception of data and promote a selective processing of events. Although they may tell part of
the story, what they do not describe—the context, history, and
motivations behind such actions—is far more important to creatively manage the conflict.

Moreover, if attribution is high, motivation to solve conflicts is
low. What commonly happens during solution seeking is that when
opponents signal that they want to offer a deal, this is attributionally
viewed as a ploy by wily adversaries to get the other side to let down
its guard. Negative attributions of aggressive dispositions and
destructive conflict are mutually self-enforcing.

The self-perceptions and attributions of opponents are often diametrically opposed. For example, the Cold War between the United
States and the Soviet Union was sustained for decades by each side
attributing aggrandizing intentions to the other side. Only when
the Soviet Union lost power and broke into pieces, thus no longer
rivaling the United States, did cooperative relationships replace the
mutual insecurity that each perceived and fostered.

Attributional bias leads to profound disconnections between messages sent and messages received in communication. In one organization an employee, Al, interpreted his boss's increasingly grumpy greetings as a reflection of his mean spirit and disregard. One morning, following such an encounter, when he finally asked his boss if he was unhappy with his performance, Al learned that the boss was simply consumed with personal problems at home; he had not even recalled seeing Al, let alone scowling at him (Mayer, 1995, p. 28).

The way we view actions and intentions depends greatly on the place from which we view them. One side says, "From where we sit, your action was one of aggression." The other responds, "To us, it was self-defense." Thus are perceptions polarized, blame perpetuated, and antagonism escalated.

Projecting. The "others" from whom we most seek to dissociate ourselves are frequently repositories of the projected elements of ourselves that we least want to accept or acknowledge.

The psychological mechanism of projection perpetuates blaming, polarizing, and negative attributions and sustains and rigidifies conflict. Projection is the universal psychological defense mechanism that people use to rid themselves of their own "shadows" such as aggression, egoism, poor judgment, and mistakes. Such characteristics are projected onto adversaries, who are construed as totally separate from the self. This serves to keep distance from the other party. "To begin again to perceive the other party as 'like self' would mean having to accept these intolerable projected parts, a very threatening situation. From this perspective, movements toward construing the other party as 'like self,' such as conciliatory gestures, are highly charged and difficult" (Northrup, 1989, p. 71).

The Us in conflicts seeks to displace any of its own aggression or morally objectionable behavior onto Them, thereby denying traits in its own group that are unacceptable. Although projection temporarily displaces the sense of guilt onto others (furthering blame), it is a form of self-deception. This is particularly true of conflicts in which disputants are so deeply intertwined that their identities are interdependent.

We project our own negative traits and aggression onto close-at-hand enemies with whom we, in fact, share much in common. We separate out the consciousness of our likeness to them because acknowledging similarity would also be acknowledging failings, blemishes, and culpability, which feel intolerable. Some of the deepest and most violent conflicts are between those close at hand. For example, most murder victims know their assailant. Ethnic conflicts are most often between people of somewhat similar stock.

Instead of owning our own issues, we project them onto others. When those others are nearby and even in many ways similar to us, the stakes are raised because distinction is more difficult and proximity more threatening. Freud described this negative enmeshment and the need for distancing as the narcissism of minor differences (1921; see also Volkan, 1988). Here it begins to become apparent why the comforting route of blaming and distinguishing Us from Them becomes very pernicious and dangerous indeed.

Antagonism in ARIA

The framing process used to articulate antagonism serves three important purposes as the starting point of the ARIA framework: it allows both sides to surface their anger and frustration in a controlled way; it allows a point of comparison for the new process about to be undertaken; and it can provide motivation for a different approach.

Because most disputants, particularly in deep and protracted conflicts, hold negative images of each other and tend to blame each other as the main cause of the conflict, the initial idea is to allow them to actively vent their anger and frustration at each other. First, they should be warned that the process may not be pleasant. However, they should also be told that it will be bounded and controlled, which will be the job of the dialogue facilitators.

Encouraging this kind of discourse flies in the face of much conventional wisdom about conflict management. Common wisdom would dictate that, at least to get things started, differences ought to be minimized and anger diffused. The danger of this approach is that unless they are allowed into the open air, these feelings will continue to fester and ultimately arise in exaggerated and uncontrollable ways. In the ARIA framework, this dialogue takes place in "islands of sanity"—retreats or workshops—away from the heat of the battle. The facilitator's job is to provide a safe haven for venting anger and setting boundaries, which will help parties observe and eventually move beyond their antagonism.

In addition, through articulating their positions the adversarial framing that disputants have used in the past becomes quite explicit. In one sense they are reciting what they have always recited, but they are now also observing the process. The idea is not simply to vent hostility but to articulate the manner in which conflicts have been played out before. Thus adversaries may become their own critical observers by watching a kind of simulation of their conflict as they reenact it.

The airing of antagonism is initially encouraged as necessary to promote consciousness of the norm, thus serving as a contrast to a better alternative that will be promoted in ensuing phases of the ARIA process. It is important to point out beforehand that this unpleasant process will be followed by a very different, more constructive reframing. With the frustration, anger, and futility of their past ways fresh in their minds, participants are generally willing to suspend their disbelief that another way might be useful. Now the groundwork has been laid to introduce a different, reflexive process and to work toward establishing a climate of resonance.

Conclusion

Conflict framing is frequently a process that results in antagonism. Left alone, adversarial framing frequently leads to an adversarial pursuit of advantage and victory. The stage is often set for new or deeper conflicts. Conflict resolution prescribes a more cooperative way of framing conflict, allowing parties to escape its cycle. Nevertheless, the ARIA framework initially encourages the expression of antagonism as necessary to promote self-consciousness of the norm. Thus it serves as a contrast for a better alternative. Moreover, such a start can also serve as a frame of reference for the critical inquiry that follows. The parties may begin to realize how the adversarial conflict framing sustains their conflict and is, in fact, a major obstacle to conflict resolution. Now is the time to offer an alternative. The stage is set to learn and choose a new way of viewing the conflict and a new path for seeking resonance and resolution.

The ARIA Quartet: Antagonism

From the beginning, like a tough-minded conductor with his orchestra, the coach takes a hard line with the quartet. After hearing a brief summary of the problem, the coach says it seems clear that the individual musicians are not being explicit about how they feel about the music or each other. "You are tiptoeing around each other and it comes through in your music. I hear little conviction, and less connection, in your playing." He asks each member of the group to be forthright about how they view the rehearsal conflict and the quartet in general. He hopes that at least he can get them to surface their concerns. "While it may feel uncomfortable to tell each other what you are feeling and thinking, please try to do so. I will ensure that things don't get out of hand. Moreover, if you are going to excel you are going to have to take some risks of openness and honesty with each other."

The musicians begin where most parties in a conflict begin—by blaming others for the difficulties. "I don't get all the fuss they make," Arthur begins, glaring at Rachel and Anthony. "We just want to get a picture of the whole piece. Then I can go off and work on my solo by myself. We know it can work if we do it this way because it's worked before."

"All we're asking is to slow down and take a closer look at passages along the way," says Rachel, the cellist. "Anthony (the violist) and I must weave in and out of this piece; often we play in the background, sometimes in the foreground, so we need the larger picture. Because you get the big moments, because you're Mr. Big Shot here, you just want to push through without forging a shared interpretation or thinking about . . ." "Anybody else," Anthony mutters. A bit taken aback, Rachel finishes, "You try to carry it all with your own charisma."

"Oh—you are just as cautious and conservative as your instruments!" Arthur retorts.

Antagonism. Each side is blaming the other, and the conflict has been set up in polarized Us versus Them terms. Now negative attributions take hold. Arthur attributes to Rachel and Anthony and their instruments, conservative, slow, and rather boring characteristics. The role of the violinists in a quartet, he asserts, is to push and take risks, and that's what makes the music great. Rachel and Anthony counter-argue that although they may often be in the background, they are the ones who carry the real burden of fine musicianship. They in return attribute to Arthur and Isabel cavalier attitudes in rehearsals and assume they selfishly care only about being in the spotlight. (Actually, Isabel is somewhat denigrated in all of this as simply Arthur's sidekick.)

What the musicians can't yet see but the coach senses is the underlying and mutually enforcing insecurities and projections felt by each player in this conflict. Although Arthur might think "I'm not sure the violist is of my caliber; maybe he's so cautious because he's not that talented," in the back of his mind is the fear that "Perhaps I push so hard because I might not be that good myself." Similarly, Rachel might be thinking, "Here I am again, in the background. Maybe that's where I truly belong." It is much less threatening to berate another for their faults than to confront one's own insecurities or limitations.

At this point the inclination of some of the musicians is simply to give up and seek other musical colleagues. But the coach pushes forward. He comforts the musicians and assures them that if they can overcome these hurdles, they stand the chance of achieving musical excellence.

3

Resonance
Articulating Common Needs and Motivations

A dramatic change takes place when we move from adversarial framing and the antagonism it generates to reflexive reframing and the resulting resonance. *Reflexive reframing* is the process during which parties articulate their own values and concerns interactively and discover common ground—or resonance.

In the process of articulating antagonistic positions, the focus is on the other, on Them, with a strong outward view. Disputants say, "You're the problem; you're the aggressive one." The focus is unidirectional; a finger points outward at the guilty one. But reflexivity is interactive. It begins from the self and gradually shifts focus to the interchange between Us and Them. An adage says that when you point your finger at someone, look where your other three fingers are pointing. In a reflexive process, attention is first given to the fingers pointing back toward oneself. Resonance with the other derives from an introspective and inward-directed exploration of questions within, about the self, rather than fixating on answers about the other.

We begin talking about ourselves—the first step in a crucial switch to reflexive reframing. The second step is to engage in dialogue with an adversary, while they too engage in open introspection about their own threatened or frustrated needs and values in a conflict. While adversarial framing fosters walls, reflexive reframing builds bridges.

In this chapter I will describe and illustrate reflexive conflict reframing and the transformative process of interactive introspection. In this process disputants speak with each other about their essential concerns, and resonance is fostered between them. This is the heart of the ARIA framework, as adversaries gain insight into what is truly at stake in a conflict and why it matters so much—respectively and interactively, within and between. As the core issues in the conflict come into focus, what can emerge transcends all separate definitions and contexts. Interactive conflict reframing, while growing out of different experiences and perceptions, is greater than all of them. It is synergistic and larger than the sum of its parts. There is a new identity waiting to be formulated in the space between disputants.

Former adversaries, by engaging in a deeply interactive reframing process, may begin to be linked by an underlying resonance emanating from the core of the conflict: namely, the identity of each party and why and how this conflict threatens and frustrates that identity. The conflict sits between them. The potential of this space in between is that it is filled by both Us and Them: We. By transforming the frame of their conflict from one of antagonism to one that resonates, parties become more *within* themselves and *between* each other. There is perhaps nothing as powerful for defining, enriching, and deepening identity as conflict over identity.

Although defining the meaning and nature of identity as a concept is no simple task, many would agree that identity itself, individual and collective, is defined by the way our lives are narrated by ourselves and others.[1] Conflict is often a powerful axis around which life stories are told. As we engage in conflict, our narratives—the way we tell our past, understand our present, and prepare for our future—often shift. The deeper the conflict, the more profound its impact on our stories. Thus identity conflicts, in addition to being formed out of our identities as they are, help to reformulate our identities as they will become. How we frame our stories, therefore, affects how our identities unfold.

When we frame the stories of our conflicts adversarially, that is, by asking Who wants what?, we establish a narrative for outcomes that each party seeks at the other's expense. The reflexive reframing process begins with an internal exploration, a new narrative, of what each side needs. It asks,

Why does who want what?

What does each side most deeply care about in this conflict, and why does it matter so much? What are their motivations? Where do the sides share responsibility for the conflict? Which needs and values are threatened or frustrated in this conflict?

Reflexivity

One of the attributes of identity conflict is its intangibility. In other words, conflict is deeply subjective; disputants locked in identity conflict often have a hard time explaining the nature of their conflict. When conflicting parties describe their dispute in terms of history, events, and significance, observers may believe they are hearing completely different histories. And they are. The subjective experience of disputants is shaped by a particular cultural reality and historical context. Moreover, disputants' experience of self and each other in conflict is also subjective. One side's freedom fighter is, after all, another side's terrorist.

Given that disputants commonly operate out of incommensurate experiences and perceptions of reality, how then can real dialogue and conflict resolution be initiated? When disputants interactively begin to go beneath the surface of their own reality and articulate the deep needs and values that are at stake for them in a conflict—exactly what matters so much—an underlying resonance is often discovered. What emerges is something larger than each separate and partial view of the conflict. It is a whole and inclusive picture.

Adversaries rarely articulate the deeper significance a conflict has for them, instead choosing to describe its outer attributes and effects. Perhaps they do not fully understand it themselves. As described in the previous chapter, conflict is commonly framed in terms of competition over limited resources—or over who wants what. As this competition hardens, opposing parties frequently blame each other and view each other with hostility and mistrust. Asking instead, *why* who wants what is a relatively uncommon but simple and effective way to reframe conflict as a vehicle for learning, growth, and cooperative action. Such an inquiry requires a reframing of positions (what outcomes parties seek) through an analysis of underlying values, priorities, and motivations (why they seek those outcomes).

Up to the Balcony

There are two forms of reflexivity. The first and most common is the automatic response to an external stimulus, akin to the physiological response that occurs when a doctor strikes a patient's knee with a mallet. Such a reflexive (knee-jerk) response to conflict is a kind of single-loop feedback between actions and reactions. It is closely tied to antagonism, when reactions are automatic and result in the classic fight-or-flight response. We either avoid the conflict by running for cover, or we strike out and try to overpower or disable the adversary.

Paradoxically, reflexivity can also mean the exact opposite. We can slow down our instinctive and unexamined reactions to an external stimulus like a conflict and analyze it, mulling over our response before we make it (Steir, 1991). We can, in William Ury's phrase, go to the balcony. "When you find yourself facing a difficult negotiation [or conflict], you need to step back, collect your wits, and see the situation objectively. Imagine you are negotiating on a stage and then imagine yourself climbing onto a balcony overlooking the stage. . . . From the balcony you can calmly evaluate the conflict, almost as if you were a third party. You can think constructively for both sides and look for a mutually satisfactory way to [frame and] resolve the problem" (Ury, 1991, p. 17). More than just a responsive act, reflexivity is a kind of "disciplined bias" by which an observer observes him- or herself observing and in the process changes that which is being observed (Soros, 1987).

This is a slowed-down and self-conscious analysis of the interactive nature of reactions. It allows us to be proactive agents in a conflict instead of reactive victims. We can then make richly informed decisions about our responses before taking action. When pointing a finger at an opponent, we might stop ourselves, count to ten, notice the remaining three fingers pointing back at ourselves and ask first, Why do I care so much?, then, What have I done to contribute to this situation?, and finally, What might I do to contribute to its creative resolution?

We can learn to encounter a conflict stimulus contemplatively, questioning our own assumptions and observing our instinctive responses. We can then disable destructive reactions when necessary and choose with care how to proceed constructively. Moving from somewhat blind assumptions and tacit reasoning, we learn to step back and observe ourselves, nurturing a profound self-awareness and volition.

This second approach to reflexivity may be boldly likened to trying to see how God sees, from all perspectives. "What would it be like if we could see each other's pictures of the history we share? If we could see each other? What we need here . . . is a little humility . . . to say 'Only God sees history whole and knows the whole truth. All I have is my perception. It's valid, it's precious, but it's fragmentary. Maybe I ought to try seeing as God sees, from all the angles.'"[2] It is a daunting charge, but indeed, this is the task of the third party, and ultimately of the conflicting parties themselves, if they are to transform negative conflicts into creative opportunities.

The Circle of Reflexivity

Single-loop reactions, like antagonistic conflict framing, are those based on a given frame that may be refined and improved, such as considering how we might better gain what we want from the other side. Double-loop decisions are based on inquiry into the nature of the frame itself, the assumptions underlying it, and whether an alternative frame might be preferable (Argyris and Schön, 1978). How might we reconceptualize our conflict so that we view all sides as in it together and therefore getting out of it together? How can we redirect the passion of our spontaneous reactions in ways that are creative instead of destructive, in ways that help us truly define and achieve our goals?

Reflexivity is circular; it turns back upon itself, changed for the journey, after traveling outward from within. The knee-jerk response is to lash out, which ultimately is self-defeating. It sets up a noose with which disputants can hang the other and themselves as well. Slowed-down reflexivity, on the other hand, can unravel the knot around the noose and enable the parties to use the rope like climbers pulling each other up the mountain.

When people begin to articulate a conflict's deep meaning to their collective identity through this process of reflexive dialogue, what becomes profoundly clear is that subjective renderings of conflict can have an intersubjective resonance between disputants. "I am afraid," says one side. "So am I," says the other. Reframing starts with introspection, shifting frames from external to internal, that is, saying "I am afraid" instead of "You are aggressive." Such a start is a necessary but insufficient first step. The next and more profound step is when disputants incorporate their different subjective frames of a conflict into a shared, intersubjective definition of their core narratives, meaning, and motives and say, "We are afraid."

Reflexivity is the mutually forming, dialectical process in which self and other significantly influence each other as mediated by some profound common experience (like identity conflict). In Buberian terms, reflexivity may be defined as the process by which an individual or group's most basic "I" (identity, values, beliefs, experiences, hopes, fears, and so on) is fundamentally articulated through an encounter with a "Thou" (Buber, [1937] 1970).

Identity conflict, even as it is often destructively construed and pursued, is also by definition formative. Such conflict contributes significantly to the constitution of disputants' respective and particular identity configurations and expressions. Unfortunately, such identity formation through the crucible of deep conflict is often reactive and negative. Identity conflict fosters polarized identities (like the early labor movement forged through bitter conflict with management); constricts identity (like managers who develop a narrow view of their role as being tough); and hardens identity ("I am because I confront management"; "I am because I control workers"). Yet identity conflict, when creatively managed, becomes more than this; it may be reflexively transformed into something else. Identity conflict also links identity— "We are we because you are you." Thus the more each side becomes itself, the more the other may evolve as well. "I am a manager in this company in part because you work here. You are a worker in this company in part because I am a manager here. So it follows that for me to be a good manager, you have to be a good worker. For you to be a good worker, I have to be a good manager. My sense of myself and my success in my job is entwined with who you are and your success."

This intersubjective (or interactive) aspect of identity in cases of identity conflict leads to a choice of continued confrontation or cooperation. Parties can continue to fight each other so that their aggressive attributes are fostered ("If they are hostile, so too must we be in return: we are because we fight"), or they may find common cause with each other to nurture their respectively higher selves ("If we are cooperative, then they may be as well: we are because we make peace").[3]

Reflexivity in Action

Reflexive reframing begins with reorienting the self (and one's primary identity group) in conflict, that is, moving from blame and victimhood to respective responsibility and volition (see Figure 3.1). Next, reframing moves from polarizing Them and Us to finding and forging common ground; Us and Them become, at least in part, We. Third, disputants get past attributing negative disposition to their adversaries. Disputants begin to gain an analytical empathy for situational constraints and understand what makes the other side tick. Finally, reflexivity leads to a shift from projecting one's own darker sides onto adversaries to acknowledging such attributes in oneself, which can lead to a profound self-awareness and ownership.

From Blame to Responsibility and Volition

In the previous chapter blame was presented as the first step in an escalating cycle of conflict. Here a way to reflexively reframe blame into respective responsibility and foster a shared will for constructive action is presented.

Given the association between blame and conflict, conflict is understandably viewed as negative and harmful. However, this is not due to conflict itself but to our attitude and approach to it. Getting beyond blame requires viewing conflict as significantly rooted within one's own side and not wholly in the space of the other side. When this is accomplished, one's relationship to conflict and to

Figure 3.1. Reflexivity in Action.

From Antagonism	To Resonance
Blaming and victimhood `- - - - - - - - - - - - - - - →`	Respective responsibility
Us versus Them `- - - - - - - - - - - - - - - - - - →`	We
Attribution `- - - - - - - - - - - - - - - - - - - - →`	Analytic empathy
Projection `- - - - - - - - - - - - - - - - - - - - - →`	Self-awareness and ownership

opponents may be viewed as a less troublesome imposition and a more creative challenge for self-awareness, volition, and self-determination. Deep conflict can richly focus the mind: it engages identity and makes identity engaging.

If blame is the first step in an escalating conflict cycle, reflexive reframing of blame can lead to conflict de-escalation, and ultimately resonance, through the promotion of a sense of mutual responsibility. Disputants can move from finger pointing to self-reflection and then on to encounter. Note the difference in the way disputants can seek to ask each other questions. Posed in impersonal, positional, or debate format, one side might ask, "Why do you insist on acting this way?" Clearly this is a statement of controversy, a stirring of antagonism. Instead, if the questioner simply makes the same question personal, from the inside out, from the self to the other, it can change the whole frame. "I feel quite put out and uncomfortable when you act this way. Is that your intention?" This is a genuine question that can begin to transform a debate into a dialogue.

Such a process can be effective even if it is unilateral. Blaming is essentially a form of accepting the status of victim and striking out at the victimizer. Viewing conflict as a learning opportunity and seeing one's side or self as at least partially responsible, at least for one's own feelings and reactions, is a balm to the vicious cycle of violence. Viewing oneself as a potential agent for change can lead to a constructive cycle of cooperation. As Buber says, "Everything depends on myself, and the critical decision: I will straighten myself out" ([1950] 1966, p. 29).[4]

With new eyes about one's own relationship to a conflict, it becomes possible to see conflict itself in a new light. Instead of viewing conflict as negative, it can instead be viewed as an ally. Rather than viewing adversaries as evil, they can be considered potential partners in a project of needed change and development. As Proust said, "The real voyage of discovery consists not in seeking new landscapes, but in having new eyes." We may still have basic differences, but our conflict can be the crucible for learning and growth.

The first step away from victimhood to volition, then, is to move from blaming the other side to looking toward one's own side, not for blame or guilt but for responsibility. How did our actions contribute to reactions by our opponents? Next, getting beyond finger pointing and distinguishing Them from Us, the reflexive approach asks parties to define for themselves and express to their opponents their own core concerns, values, and needs that are at stake in the conflict. Simultaneously, the reflexive process is used to guide them to truly listen to each other's expression of deep motives, needs, and values and discover resonance.

By switching conflict frames from external blaming to internal inquiry, the dialectical and reflexive nature of conflict begins to reveal itself. Conflict reframing becomes possible. No longer is conflict something out there, something They have done to Us. Instead, it is something interactive. "You are in conflict with me because I am in conflict with you, and I am in conflict with you because you are in conflict with me. What might we do about this, separately and together?" This approach to conflict is profoundly democratizing. Through such an analysis, the conflict playing field may be leveled. Even when one party is significantly stronger than another, through economic or military power, for example, the process of conflict transformation itself can be a leveler.[5] Both sides may come to realize that they need the other side if their destructive conflict is to become constructive. If either coercion or conquest is ultimately ineffective or impossible, then something else is required—cooperation.

Cooperation, development, and creative imagination are the common output of the journey of conflict viewed from the inside out. In short, viewing conflict as potentially useful can help make it so. Viewing adversaries as potential allies can help make them so.

From Us Versus Them to We

In Chapter Two it was suggested that an Us-against-Them mentality is required for perpetuating blame; it is also self-fulfilling.

Here a way is presented to reframe such polarization into convergence: We.

If opponents have sharply distinguished themselves from each other through blame and polarization, they will be unable to hear or accept the other's definition of the conflict they share. It is common for disputants to totally "miss" each other when they speak about their conflict.

Reflexive reframing requires that disputants be able to understand the interactive nature of their conflict. This means they must be able to move away from blame and polarizing to discover a common frame of reference. The discovery of this convergence requires that conflicting parties understand the context and deep motivations for the thoughts and deeds of the other side, as well as their own. Fostering a common frame can significantly contribute to transforming intransigent conflict from recurring crisis to new opportunity.

Once conflict positions have been staked out in an antagonistic way, the Why? question is all too rarely asked. When it *is* asked, it is often done belligerently, as in, "Why have you been so aggressive?" and responses are then in-kind: "Because you backed us into a corner." The search for motivations beyond blame and counter-blame is an essential but rare process. It requires a new way of analyzing and exploring conflict, one that may disable or transcend defensive reactions and encourage shared inquiry. In a sense, a process of collaborative research by opponents into the sources and conditions behind a conflict cycle is required.

Creative reflexivity in deep conflict situations can do this. It leads parties to articulate their own underlying motivations and needs in a conflict. Hearing each other speak about deep needs and values, disputants in identity conflicts regularly discover common concerns. They may begin to speak interactively of We instead of Us and Them and begin to reformat the conflict issues—why they matter so much, why they hurt so much. This can generate a new focus for analysis and discourse by zeroing in on which core values, hopes, and fears are at stake and which needs are threatened and frustrated. In articulating their own deep narratives through this kind of interactive introspection, disputants can begin to hear overlapping stories of joys and sorrows, hopes and fears, needs and motivations, and begin to discover places in the other side's tale that powerfully merge and mesh with their own. A disputant may say, "We have sought control over our destiny above all else; it seems that they too have been driven by a similar motive."

Through such a process, conflicting parties may find ways to stop viewing every interaction with their adversaries as a competition. Instead, conditions are fostered for creative analysis and discussion between adversaries. After articulating their own situation reflexively and hearing their opponents do the same, they often discover a deep, intersubjective meshing of stories: My story and your story equals our story (Bruner, 1987).

From Negative Attribution to Analytic Empathy

In the previous chapter the pernicious role of attributions in conflict escalation was discussed: everything bad they do against us is innate and characteristic; everything we do against them is reactive and situational. Getting out of this closed-minded perspective requires a new analysis of motivation and causation. "Analytic empathy" is here presented as a vehicle to enable disputants to view each other's aggression as at least partially similar to their own—as reactively motivated due to threats and frustrations of essential needs and values. This reframe provides the opportunity for forging new cooperative relationships for addressing such threats and frustrations at their sources.

If we can come to accept that our opponents may act out of motivations as complex and multidimensional as our own, we can also learn to differentiate between bad acts and bad people. Just as we believe that many of our aggressive reactions to others are situationally motivated and not due to innate character flaws, so we may begin to see that perhaps many of the aggressive actions of our adversaries also are reactively linked to circumstances. Circumstances can be changed. Character, on the other hand, is much more firmly rooted. Although we can never come to see the world as our adversaries do, nor necessarily accept their assertions as correct, we can begin to understand their viewpoints and assumptions as contextually legitimate. On that basis we may be able to identify those on the other side with whom common cause might well be formulated.

Reflexivity can be a very powerful tool in challenging negative attributions and changing the context of how a conflict is defined. How each side defines a conflict is inextricably linked to its understanding of the context. Therefore it follows that the contextual understanding of a conflict dictates the way parties will respond. As the conflict theorist Anthony de Reuck aptly observed, "Action and communication are understood only by reading the *content* of each in light of its *context* (or frame). It is as though every message were a cablegram which bore at the beginning (as most cablegrams do) a further message about who was the sender, to whom it was sent, and the code that should be used to interpret it" (1990, p. 191).

The purpose of an exchange of information about essential concerns between disputants is to create that context and foster an analytic understanding of commonalties. I term such an understanding *analytic empathy* (Rothman, 1992). Ralph White speaks of *realistic empathy* (1984). This is quite different from *emotional empathy*, when parties come to feel like one another. Instead, analytic empathy creates an ability for parties to identify similarities between their own side and that of their adversaries. This may guide them away from previous negative attributions of the other. Overcoming negative dispositional attributions and gaining analytic empathy may help considerably in breaking the vicious conflict cycle in which each negative act of the other side is interpreted as confirmation of their evil nature and intentions.

Through a reflexive dialogue, parties may begin to see that just as they themselves have acted in part due to situational determinants ("We felt threatened, therefore we engaged in preemptive strikes"), so too the other side has acted upon such motives ("After

our attack they felt threatened and they retaliated in hopes of preventing further strikes"). This is a major step toward conflict de-
escalation and forging resonance.

Such analytic empathy can lead parties to accept that the other
side, in ways quite similar to one's own, is deeply motivated to fulfill underlying needs and fully express their own values, to overcome
past traumas, and to ensure future safety. They may begin to realize
that coercion or suppression of those needs and values is likely to be
counter-productive. Such analytic empathy can serve as a more solid
foundation for joint problem solving based on hard-headed calcula-
tions of its necessity—for one's own side. "Since we can't avoid
them, beat them, ultimately suppress them, or even eventually conquer them, and since they are as determined as we are to fulfill their
needs and values, perhaps we had better find ways to cooperate."

To gain analytic empathy for one another, all sides must speak
honestly and openly about their hopes, hurts, and motivations. One
useful framework for helping parties reflexively reframe their conflict and speak truthfully is through the vehicle of a universal "needs
analysis." Abraham Maslow, an early theorist who hypothesized the
role of needs in human relations and motivations, suggested a conceptual framework for human motivations that he labeled a "hierarchy of needs" (Maslow, 1943, pp. 370–396). Maslow suggests that
all human beings, irrespective of context, class, or culture, seek to
fulfill their needs hierarchically. First, humans seek to satisfy their
most basic physiological needs for food and shelter, next for safety
and security, next for love and belongingness, next for self-esteem,
and finally for self-actualization.

Others, like Paul Sites and John Burton, suggest that all humans
seek to fulfill all their needs simultaneously—needs for response, security, recognition, stimulation, distributive justice, meaning, rationality, and control over their own destiny (Burton, 1990a). It is difficult
if not impossible to prove the existence of either a hierarchy of needs
or the specific types and forms of needs that are presented as univer-
sally shared.[6] The main point of a needs analysis in deep conflict is

that it provides a common conceptual framework to use in articulating and organizing the motivations of those locked in the conflict. Moreover, by suggesting that needs are universal and that threats to basic needs and frustration over unmet needs are at the root of intransigent conflicts, a new type of analytic discourse about conflict motivations replaces polemical positional discourse about solutions. This new discourse can help foster a common conflict frame.

Safety is a good example of a need that is clearly felt by all and is not a limited resource. The safer one side feels, the more likely it is to afford security to another. In fact most needs are expansive by nature. The more they are fulfilled for one party, the more another party may achieve them. In a labor dispute that had gone on for years, by reframing the conflict with a new sensitivity to its causes—threats to efficacy, safety, recognition, dignity, and the perpetuation of mutual insecurity and mistrust—union and management began to break their conflict cycle and chart new ways to cooperatively address their differences (see Chapter Seven).

In gaining analytic empathy for why the other side has acted as it has, parties may begin to develop a sense that their opponents are indeed "like self." It becomes clear that both sides have some of the same situational constraints and underlying motivations for fulfilling needs like safety, control, and identity. "You have felt threatened and thus acted in a way we perceived as aggressive, so we too have been aggressive in response to a real or perceived threat, and you too have perceived us as aggressive." This affords a broadening of identity, which may facilitate a breakdown of the absolute Us versus Them split so common in deep conflict. Ideally this split is replaced with "a construct that defines all others as at least partially like-self" (Northrup, 1989, p. 80).

From Projection to Self-Awareness

In the previous chapter the projection process in sustaining and deepening conflict was presented. It described how "others" from whom we most seek to dissociate ourselves are frequently repositories of the projected elements of ourselves that we least want to accept or acknowledge. Here it will be shown that making peace with "external" adversaries often requires making peace with "internal" foes first.

Our shadows are also part of ourselves, both personal and collective (Jung, 1953). In seeking to expel them, disown them, ignore them, or project them, we get deeply entangled by our darker selves. When we encounter them from without, our buttons are pushed, and our reactions are usually disproportionate to the stimulus. In making peace with the fact that we are imperfect, human, and fallible, we may begin to gain more control over our own shadow sides. In addition to acknowledging and articulating our own motivations in a conflict, coming to terms with the psychological origins within our own hearts of some of our antipathy for our adversaries can provide us with a very powerful self-awareness. We learn to face and own aspects of ourselves we would rather not acknowledge. We can then make mature decisions about what to do with them rather than play the ventriloquist's game of falsely throwing our voice onto a mannequin of our own construction.

In an intervention in an organization rife with blame and attribution where a new scapegoat was selected on a regular basis (after the previous one had been sent over a cliff), a consultant asked a group of managers to divide a piece of paper in two. They were instructed to write down on one side attributes of another manager who really "bugged" them. After they had completed this task, they were instructed to write on the other side some attributes of themselves that they did not admire. On comparison, many were surprised to find much that overlapped across the two sides of the sheet. "Moreover," said one, "I find that some of the things that bug me about the person are not only negatives. They also include things I envy."

If the "other" becomes the repository of all things bad, some form of belittlement or dehumanization of the adversary is psychologically conditioned. To disable these blinding projections, the parties need to strive instead for awareness of which aspects of the other side really push their buttons. It is common wisdom that when something about someone else really bothers you, you can often find traces of your antipathy toward others in yourself.

Conclusion

In reflexive dialogue, disputants reframe their perceptions and analyses of each other and their own identities. Where blame was, mutual responsibility enters. Where an Us-versus-Them dynamic prevailed, there develops an understanding of the way all disputants have been locked into a relationship and have been, in part, defined by it. Through interactive introspection, this creates the potential for the new use of the concept of We. Where negative attributions clouded all differentiation of the others, a new analytic empathy may emerge in which they are viewed as "like self" in certain deeply motivated needs and values such as safety and dignity. Finally, where pernicious projections were entrenched, a new awareness of a disputant's own imperfections is acknowledged and accepted, promoting a less self-righteous or judgmental battle and more tolerance for failings of the other side as well.

Kurt Lewin in his classic book, *Resolving Social Conflicts* (1948), suggests that when disputants are locked in bitter battles, they must somehow "unfreeze" cognitions about each other and the situations that perpetuate the fight. Indeed conflict can be the gift that thaws those perceptions by propelling everyone involved to become reflexive. Reflexivity demands that we clarify why we care so much about issues and leads us to listen to why others care so much as well. This allows a fresh view, fosters resonance, and prepares the way for cooperative and integrative problem solving.

Reflexivity creates something that was not there before. One can think of a violin as nothing more than some pieces of wood with a few animal hairs strung about. But in the hands of the right person, it can make beautiful music. Add another musician and they respectively may make each other better. Moreover, many musicians will tell you that it takes an inspired audience to make an inspired performance. What is an audience but some people sitting on chairs listening? Nevertheless there is a powerful energy that can flow within and between an audience and musicians that transforms each into a greater, deeper entity than they were before. Separately they are just some people playing and some people listening. Together they make music.

The ARIA Quartet: Resonance

The coach knows that if this quartet is to truly make music, all members must arrive at a place of resonance. Operating in the reflexive mode, the coach's next job is to get the musicians to look at their conflict in a different way, focusing not on blaming and negative attribution but on the underlying needs and values they hold in common.

When confronted with the accusation that he is hiding something, Arthur, the first violinist, finds himself on the verge of tears. "I feel like my integrity is on the line. I feel like you are judging me as a dishonest person, accusing me of intentionally playing false notes," he says. Arthur is surprised at his own feelings simply from being told he was hiding. Now is the time to explore why this conflict raises such emotions for Arthur. It is time to ask what matters so much to these musicians, and *why*? Through an intense period of reflexivity, the members of this quartet may find that they essentially seek the same goals, despite their differing approaches and personalities.

At this point the coach suggests that the problem with the quartet is not that some want to rehearse one way and the others want to do it a different way. The problem is that they are not finding a way to mesh their differences.

After listening to further explanations of how each musician approaches his or her art, it becomes clear to the coach that they share many common needs. All are trying to create great music as a means of achieving recognition in their field. All feel the need to maintain a large measure of control over their art. Not surprisingly, given the recent formation of this group, there is also a good deal of insecurity swirling around along with the notes, with bravado serving as a facade. Through his insistence, the coach manages to move the group slowly from polarization to resonance. "This group will not survive in an environment of first-tier versus second-tier musicians," he insists. "In a group of four, if you're not playing with a deep and abiding unity, paradoxically employing your diversity to do so, there is no way you will ever achieve greatness. You need to find a path that meets the needs of each member, or your quartet is destined to be quartered."

Slowly, Arthur turns reflexive. "Maybe I am partially responsible for this conflict. I admit my style may turn some people off, but it's how I try to push myself to do better. I will try to make peace by beginning to listen to your desire for musical interpretation," he says, looking at Rachel. "I admit that part of the reason I haven't wanted to perform my solos in front of you is because I fear your negative criticism, but I do recognize that my work is ultimately part of the whole."

Anthony, the violist chimes in. "You're right that we are interested in your solos because they reflect on the group as a whole. Let us show you that we can comment on and inquire into your work in a way that is helpful and supportive."

Rachel, the cellist takes the discussion one step further. "I know that as a violinist, you want to be great. I respect that. We want to be great too, not as soloists but as an ensemble. I want to be true to this great music. For us to be great, I feel that we as a group must carefully consider every step we take."

Here the coach points out that a common need for greatness and recognition is apparent. "You may have different styles, but you both say you want to be great," he says.

"Yes," agrees Rachel. "Maybe his brashness and speed is not simply arrogance but his vision of what it is to be great."

"And maybe," Arthur adds, "you believe that recognition comes from truth to the music. You believe that by carefully probing into Brahms, you will receive recognition as a fine interpreter."

"Perhaps you are just following different paths toward greatness and recognition," the coach gently coaxes.

This discussion does not magically end the clash in rehearsal styles. But it does illuminate common underlying needs among the musicians for control and recognition, and a shared sense of insecurity. Through the articulation of what is really at stake, it has become apparent that this quartet, if it is to survive and thrive, must find a way to give all its members a sense of voice, recognition, control, and security. They need to develop a new style and identity—one that encompasses all their identities.

4

Invention

Generating Cooperative Solutions

A Middle Eastern parable: A man died, leaving seventeen camels to his three sons. The first son was to receive one-half, the second son was to receive one-third, and the third son was to receive one-ninth. They were unable to figure out how to divide the camels fairly. After arguing among themselves, they consulted a wise old woman for a solution to this difficult problem. She offered to lend them her one camel. Of the eighteen camels, the first son took nine, the second took six, and the third son took two. One camel was left over, so the sons gave it back to the woman.

This chapter is about making peace pay. Presentation of the ARIA framework turns now to the process of inventing solutions that go beyond the normal concepts of domination or compromise. To develop and nurture these inventions, it is essential to move from reframing to creative imagination. Having reframed deep conflict and perceiving it now as a source of potential resonance, the task ahead is to make that perception self-fulfilling.

Albert Einstein aptly observed that the "formulation of a problem is often more essential than its solution." One way to invent creative solutions to problems that have been reframed is to go outside of normal paradigms. Adversarial modes of negotiation and problem solving are not effective with identity conflicts. Instead, a whole new approach is needed. The following illustration is one classic example of how creative solutions call upon a new and different outlook. The task is to connect all nine dots by drawing just four lines without taking the pencil off the paper:

○   ○   ○

○   ○   ○

○   ○   ○

This is quite an impossible problem to solve using traditional ideas about finding solutions. Creative imagination and invention often require going outside the box.

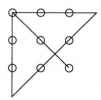

In traditional conflict management, compromise is considered a good outcome. It certainly is an advance over win-lose methods. If the problems being addressed are indeed primarily about scarce resources like territory or money, then exploring mutual concessions is often necessary and appropriate. If the problems, at least at their core, are about identity and human needs, then discussing losses and compromise at the outset can easily stop creative problem solving before it starts. Compromise becomes a problem when people come to believe that working with the other side leads to giving up what they find most essential. Conversely, if they can begin to feel that cooperation with the other side is going to lead to the further fulfillment of their needs and values, then working with the other side becomes very attractive.

In addition to developing new mental models about the nature of conflict—from something inherently negative to something potentially positive—new ideas about the meaning of solutions are also required. Before parties locked in intransigent conflict can imagine an interactive process of problem solving, it is first necessary to shift their perception of the outcomes of such a process from that of zero-sum (The more the other side gains, the more I lose) to that which is potentially positive-sum (The more the other side gains, the more I may gain as well). When deep human motivations are at the heart of conflicts, solutions must be formulated and pursued, at least initially, in ways that focus on potential gains rather than sacrifices. In short, peace must be seen to pay.

This is the time in conflict resolution to switch to a more applied voice. How, after all, might conflicts over identity, dignity, and survival be practically addressed if not through very concrete and daily issues like economics, security arrangements, environmental resources, and so forth? This is also the time to use practical tools in the search for new ways to solve problems. The inventing process is about developing concrete solutions to bring resonance to life and serves to consolidate and give concrete form to new insights about each other and the conflict. A new understanding of interdependence and its positive potential can replace fighting and antagonism. It should be clear to everyone by now that all disputants are in the conflict together, and they have to get out of it together.

Where reflexive reframing fosters a new conceptual foundation of identity conflict as a shared opportunity for development and needs fulfillment, the inventing process must begin the actual construction of a new edifice. As is often the case in complex undertakings like transforming conflict into creativity, the devil is in the details.

From Formula to Detail

To consolidate this new way of seeing conflict, the inventing process promotes cooperation in concrete ways, both in means and ends. This is akin to what Zartman and Berman (1982) describe as a necessary progression in problem solving and negotiations from formula to detail (see Figure 4.1). Formulas are broad statements of objectives. They may be derived from reframing and can help parties gain

Figure 4.1. From Formula to Detail.

What and *Why* (formula)	Problem as reframed in terms of shared motives and needs
↓	↓
How (detail)	Integrative frameworks to address problems cooperatively

understanding as to why who should get what, in terms of their underlying concerns for safety, identity, dignity, and so forth. From formulas, parties must now address details about adopting specific steps, stages, and strategies—in short, the *how* necessary for new formulas to have lasting and practical effects.

The first step in applying the new will to fulfill common needs articulated during reflexive reframing is to address such needs through detailed inventions. It is perhaps impossible to actually negotiate a deal about parties' underlying motivations, beyond the crucial and often difficult phase of moving from mutual rejection to mutual recognition. Underlying and shared motivations have to be converted into practical steps and strategies and translated into concrete and functional terms. If a party expresses a need for greater safety, for example, this can be concretely pursued in terms of tangible security measures. If a party expresses a need to assert its identity more fully, then educational or cultural vehicles may be useful expressions of such identity needs. If a party expresses a need for greater control over its destiny, new modes of political or organizational participation or economic development may be designed. These instrumental mechanisms, or means, may be summarized as *functional interests*.

This definition of interests is somewhat idiosyncratic to the model developed in this book; it modifies the usual concept of interests as ends in themselves, such as "in the national interest" (Morgenthau, 1948), or shared interests beneath exclusive positions (Fisher and Ury, 1981). Promoting "interest-based" or "principled bargaining" to replace "positional bargaining," Fisher and Ury and other negotiation theorists suggest that interests are primary motivators of all conflicts; thus creatively addressing parties' underlying interests will go far in managing them. This appears to be accurate in describing resource-based conflicts. However, when conflicts are over fundamental human concerns, interests may be more accurately described as functional means or vehicles—like education or security mechanisms—for promoting or protecting such deep concerns.

Though often blurred, a distinction between interests and needs is a useful one, as is the distinction between resource and identity conflicts, for determining when which types of solution strategies should be used.[1] In resource-driven conflicts, interests are regularly prime motivators, and thus bargaining and compromise are often effective. In identity conflicts, interests may become useful means for fulfilling needs; however, they are not ends in themselves as they are in resource conflicts. Although interests in a tangible conflict and interests in an existential conflict might look alike (greater economic well-being, for example), in resource conflicts they are the ends themselves; in identity conflicts they are a means to an end. Distinguishing when disputants are really fighting over money and when they are fighting over needs that money represents is crucial for determining the best course of action in addressing the conflict.

Another limitation with interest-based bargaining for addressing identity conflicts is that while it seeks to get parties to move off positions and focus on interests, it is common for disputants to view interests as means of fulfilling their original positions. For example, instead of fighting about political control over Jerusalem, Israelis and Palestinians are counseled to find shared interests, like economic development, that they can work to achieve cooperatively. The problem is that each side is likely to view economic development as a means to shoring up their political claims over Jerusalem. In the ARIA approach, having reframed problems from positions to needs, interests become a means of fulfilling the needs at stake (see Figure 4.2). Thus when Israelis and Palestinians agree to cooperate economically,

Figure 4.2. From Positions to Needs to Interests.

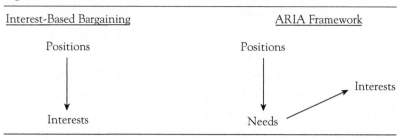

it is not in order to jockey for position when it comes to "final status" negotiations over Jerusalem. Instead economic development is viewed as an effective means of fulfilling such basic needs as control over destiny and well-being (see Chapter Six).

The idea of interests is still useful as a building block in developing a strategy for solving identity conflicts. It implies a sense of concrete, practical, and functional concerns in common parlance. In fact if one thinks about the way interests are usually conceptualized, the functional focus on interests as means is not a major departure. It is rather a new emphasis. The ARIA approach, rooted in an analysis of threats and frustrations to identity needs, shifts to solution seeking by examining what interests (or means) should be cooperatively pursued to address the needs of all disputants.

Cooperative Strategies and Outcomes

To address interests as a means of fulfilling needs in a collaborative way, disputants must learn strategies for problem solving in which all parties benefit. The primary aim of inventing such solutions is to build confidence that cooperation is useful and can and should be launched and sustained. One approach that is still relatively unknown in the international arena but more developed theoretically and practically in industrial relations is the integrative approach to problem solving. This framework was first formulated by Mary Parker Follet and refers to strategies and options by which parties can cooperatively solve their conflicts with each other. "There are three main ways of dealing with conflict: domination, compromise, and integration. Domination, obviously, is a victory of one side over the other. . . . Compromise [occurs when] each side gives up a little in order to have peace. . . . [Integration occurs when] a solution has been found in which both desires have found a place, [such] that neither side has to sacrifice anything" (Follet, 1941, p. 32).

To the extent that parties continue to frame their conflicts in terms of opposing positions—all or nothing—domination strategies resulting in winners and losers are inevitable. As previously discussed, the way problems are formulated and framed significantly influences the choices people make in trying to solve them. Once parties determine that their underlying needs are central causes of their conflicts, they may be on their way to discovering overlapping concerns for which cooperative approaches are far more effective than competitive ones.

An integration of parties' interests is especially necessary when neither side will sacrifice anything it really needs; integration thus enables parties to work together to fulfill their own needs without undermining those of the other. The 1978 Camp David Peace Talks mediated by U.S. President Jimmy Carter provide a clear example of going beyond positions to integrating interests in order to fulfill needs. When negotiators from Egypt and from Israel met at Camp David, Maryland, their conflict appeared intractable. Egypt demanded the immediate return of the entire Sinai Peninsula. Israel, which had occupied the Sinai since 1967, wanted to maintain it as a buffer zone. Proposals based on compromise were unacceptable to both sides. As long as the conflict was defined in terms of the amount of land each would control, no agreement could be reached. The impasse from these positions was broken with a new focus on underlying national needs. Israel was concerned about the security that the Sinai offered. Egypt's primary concern was its sovereignty over the Sinai and regaining lost national dignity and prestige. The parties agreed upon the return of the Sinai to Egypt, in exchange for assurances of a demilitarized area and funds from the United States for moving Israeli air bases and rebuilding them in the Negev desert. This functional and interest-based solution met the underlying needs—for safety and dignity—of each side.

In another example, a labor union needing to feel that it is getting a fair shake seeks to participate in the hard decision-making process that will be necessary to keep the company afloat. Management needs to feel that it is able to ensure the company's survival and wants to be sure that labor will not hurt its odds. Through joint problem reframing it can become clear to both sides that their respective needs are not really in conflict. On the contrary, they are interdependent. If appropriate strategies are applied, mutual gains can be achieved and needs fulfilled.

Such achievement, however, does not necessarily mean that everyone gets everything desired. Disputants may come to realize that while they can't always get everything they want, if they try real hard they can perhaps, through cooperation and integrative problem solving, get what they truly need. In recent years there has been a popularization of a notion that win-win solutions are the ideal outcome of a conflict. In reality such a goal is often unrealistic.[2] Instead it is enough if sides in a conflict seek to undertake mutual accommodations and cooperative efforts in good faith with a view toward ensuring the fulfillment of the underlying needs of all parties.

Instead of asking, How can I maximize my gains and minimize my losses? parties now begin to ask, How can all sides collaborate to maximize our gains and agree on mutual adjustments so that our gains can be assured and our needs fulfilled? Collaborative tactics reflect parties' mutual rather than separate orientation. "Collaborative tactics involve a stance toward conflict management very different from competitive tactics. A competitive tactic assumes that the size of the pie is finite; therefore, one's tactics are designed to maximize gains for oneself and losses for the other. Collaborative tactics, however, assume that the size of a pie can be increased by working with the other party" (Hocker and Wilmot, 1995, p. 111).

Cooperative Problem-Solving Techniques

Many integrative techniques have been widely applied in recent decades at the level of industrial relations, and to some extent they are beginning to be applied in the international arena as well.[3] To facilitate problem solving, disputants who are engaged in an inventing process may find three varieties of integrative solutions particularly useful: *differentiation, expansion,* and *compensation.* Though by no means exhaustive of integrative approaches, these three approaches are useful in developing a new mind-set about integrative solution seeking and moving away from concepts of domination, and particularly away from compromise. They may be viewed as aids in stepping outside the box and guiding a process of creative invention.

A classic example of interest-based bargaining is the story of the conflict over an orange (adapted from Fisher and Ury, 1981). Two sisters want an orange, but there is only one orange available. After a brief argument about who wants and deserves the orange more, the sisters decide to try to work out their conflict in a more rational way. They begin to talk about why they respectively *need* the orange. One reminds the other of her health problem and of the fact that her doctor has told her to drink fresh-squeezed orange juice daily. The other, a baker, says she needs the peel for her special orange cake. "This is one of the best cakes I make," she says, "and it doesn't work without real oranges." "But my doctor told me I need oranges," responds the other sister. "I'm afraid I'll get sick if I don't have the orange." She communicates her underlying need in this conflict—a need for well-being. For the baker, the orange is tied in with her sense of her craft, and ultimately, her creativity.

Differentiation

When parties' interests in a conflict appear to differ significantly, differentiation techniques can be used in an effort to build integrative solutions.

Once the sisters have articulated their underlying needs in the conflict over the orange, they discover they have different interests: one for the peel, the other for the juice. Thus they can divide the orange, yet neither side has to compromise (see Figure 4.3).

In one labor-management conflict, I had to find a way to get beneath the usual battle over wages. It became clear that management's motivation in the conflict was fostering stability in a system that had just endured major upheavals and turbulence; the union was motivated by a concern for greater recognition for its people, who had also suffered the indignities and blows of belt-tightening and insecurity about the future. Differentiation was used to good effect to promote renewed trust and cooperation, helping to build a foundation for more cooperative negotiations over wages and benefits in the future. Management sought to have fewer costly grievances filed; the union's aim was to have problems handled more proactively and with the active participation of union leaders. Different concerns led to a shared outcome.

Expansion

Using expansion techniques, parties attempt to enlarge the amount, type, or use of available resources.

Returning to the example of the orange, if the sisters decide that they both need the whole orange, employing the passion and energy otherwise diverted by conflict, they might explore avenues for locating another orange (see Figure 4.4).

By using expansion, it may be possible to develop an already existing resource (for example, developing additional sources of

Figure 4.3. Solving the Orange Conflict: Differentiation.

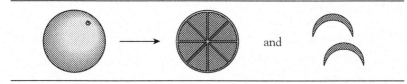

and

water); different types of resources can be added (using economic aid to add water lines); or a new use of an existing resource can be cultivated (expanding energy resources for improved efficiency in water distribution). Competing for water may actually decrease the overall supply, whereas cooperative efforts may lead to greater development and wiser usage of existing resources.

The notion of integrative processes requires that disputants come to positively recognize their interdependence. One of the most powerful means of preparing for integrative problem solving, particularly expansion, is through the discovery or creation of "superordinate goals." Sherif illustrated this in his famous Robbers Cave experiment. When two previously competing groups of summer campers had to get a food truck out of the mud or face no supper, they found cooperation to be the only way to do it. Finding themselves positively interdependent, they began to overcome many of their intergroup rivalries (Sherif and others, 1961). In order to be effective, superordinate goals must have high appeal for all parties and must be beyond the means of any party to achieve by themselves.

Despite their physical or psychic proximity, or in part due to it, disputants often have had very little positive contact with each other. Thus in addition to reaching superordinate goals, or in order to promote them, it can be helpful to structure cross-cutting activities. Through informal social gatherings between labor and management, youth encounters, or shared sports and educational activities, for example, disputants are able to interact positively. This helps reduce stereotypes and humanizes the other side. Such positive contact can provide much grist for the cooperation mill.

Figure 4.4. Solving the Orange Conflict: Expansion.

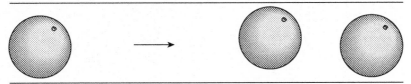

Compensation

To use compensation techniques to promote integrative solutions, parties must first determine the extent to which they differentiate their needs or interests. They can then offer exchanges or provide compensation for issues and interests they value differently.

In the case of the orange, the sisters may discover that they prioritize the value of the orange differently. Because one sister needs to drink her juice soon, and the baker decides she can wait several hours to make her cake, they agree that the first sister's need is more immediate. They decide that she will get the orange and give the other some money (worth more than the price of a single orange) to compensate her for the trouble of having to go buy another one (see Figure 4.5).

In a conflict between an embattled superintendent and his school board, a form of noneconomic compensation was used to get beyond the Us-versus-Them split and foster a common cause in a rebuilding effort. The board compensated the superintendent, who had seriously considered resigning; compensation was not in money but in a promise to be more supportive of him and vigilant against those in the community making political capital at his expense. He, in turn, promised to stay and rededicate himself to the system.

Incremental gains, or "pieces of peace," that one side may offer the other in exchange for something else, can be powerful in fostering confidence and advancing the constructive cycle of cooperation.

An illustration of a conflict between a worker and his boss will be helpful in showing how integrative techniques might work.

Figure 4.5. Solving the Orange Conflict: Compensation.

Frank, a midlevel manager, storms into his boss's office without knocking. He feels his boss has undermined him in front of a client one time too many. But before Frank can get a word out, Susan, his boss, coldly stakes out her position. "This is the last time I'm putting up with this behavior. You're fired." At which point Frank shouts, "You can't do that. I quit!"

When calmer heads finally prevail, Frank and Susan agree to go over their dispute with a third party they both trust. They hold a reflexive dialogue about what is really at stake for them in this conflict and why it matters so much. For Susan it is dignity and respect in her role as head of the firm, and for Frank it is recognition. With this new understanding, they try to work out new ways to improve their working relationship.

Differentiation

Frank and Susan discover that their needs are really not in conflict with each other. Susan requires dignity and the knowledge that she is respected in her role as the head of the firm. Frank expresses his need for recognition that he is a valuable member of the firm whose opinions matter. They decide to create a new job description for Frank, one that gives him a new role and a new sense of self in the firm. "However, you need to understand that the buck stops with me. I am the person who has to make the decisions to keep this company alive. If you can't live with that, I don't see how we can work together." Frank responds, "Thank you. I can live with that." Susan ends by telling Frank she is grateful for his participation in their discussions. "I could tell you were furious, but I just couldn't figure out what it was about."

Expansion

The initial hostility and passion in their blow-up surprises both Frank and Susan. Once they are able to cool off and hold a civil discussion, they both discover that the passion of their argument represents a deep commitment to the firm. Once he decides he cannot tolerate the idea of leaving his job, Frank pledges himself to finding a way to make it work with Susan. Their reflexive discussion leads to a sense of synergy, a sense that they can merge their separate strengths to create a firm that is better than either of them only because it includes both of them. They commit their separate egos and identities to working together to pull the load. Previously dreading their weekly meetings, they now both look forward to them as times to invent ways to grow the firm together.

Compensation

Although Frank ultimately does receive a raise in his new position at the firm, it is not the most important form of compensation that comes out of this conflict with Susan. In his discussions with her, Frank indicates that although he does believe he deserves a higher salary, it is more important to him to be given greater responsibility and increased authority. Susan agrees to that, provided it is accompanied by Frank affording her more respect. She says, "You are a very valued manager here, and I want your ideas and input." Frank responds, "Thanks. While it may not seem like it sometimes, I think you are a fine CEO and plan to offer you my support and appreciation more than I have lately."

Momentum

Just as nothing succeeds like success, nothing gets parties in conflict engaged in a conflict management process more quickly than constructive momentum. The vicious cycle of violence and aggression is a well-known phenomenon. Once launched, aggression develops a life of its own that is hard to stop. The constructive cycle of cooperation is experienced far less often but may be equally powerful; certainly it is more creative. When conflict is converted into cooperation, a new kind of dynamic energy is released and can be quite contagious.

The pieces of peace that disputants construct with one another through integrative techniques can have a snowball effect; they are big enough to matter but initially small enough to work. When parties begin down a path of cooperation and gain something in return—new partners, greater benefits, more security, a new confidence that problems can actually be solved—their internal commitment to that path increases. In a speech just minutes before his assassination in 1995, Israeli Prime Minister Yitzhak Rabin, known for much of his life as a hard-headed military man of few words, spoke about the self-propelling dynamics of cooperation that he had helped to launch with the Arab world. He said, "Peace is amazing!"

Conclusion

In attempting to promote integrative inventions, it is important to generate as many options as possible. One of the benefits of a preparatory phase prior to formal negotiation or problem solving is that options are generated in an exploratory and nonbinding way. Producing a wide range of creative and cooperative possibilities for subsequent use fosters confidence in the value of further cooperation. Following the development of a wide range of alternatives, the parties can evaluate the inventions in light of the list of underlying needs they have developed during reframing. They are then able to assess the extent to which the options, if implemented, would be acceptable to constituencies on both sides.

Inventing is the process through which integrative approaches are used to design mutually acceptable solutions to a conflict whereby all sides gain. This builds confidence that negotiations are worth undertaking. Moreover, this approach also cultivates agreements that last. It helps overcome a dilemma that often arises when parties are forced, through distributive techniques, into concessions. The "winners" frequently do not retain their "spoils" for very long because the "losers" are not content with what they have achieved through the negotiation. The ARIA framework strives for the feeling that all sides have won with regard to the issues with which they are most concerned.

The ARIA Quartet: Inventing

The coach now guides the discussion toward inventing solutions that will fulfill the needs of each quartet member and of the group. He suggests that although compromise might seem to be the simplest and easiest way out, it is often counter-productive when deep concerns are at stake. "Your music is an expression of your selves; the way you seek to make your music is part of who you are as well," he says. "Therefore, instead of a normal give and take approach, perhaps you can find one in which your various approaches resonate with each other."

He asks the group to brainstorm possible solutions to their conflict—inventions that might lead them to a new synergy. As an example, the coach suggests it might be possible to try rehearsing both ways. "Without compromising your need to perfect your solos," he says to Arthur, the first violinist, "could you also emphasize the voice of the group?" To the cellist, Rachel, he proposes, "In addition to seeking to master the various nuances of the piece, could you try several run-throughs in which you see that a key role for you is to support Arthur?"

Several members of the quartet say this seems to be simply a compromise. But the coach stresses that it is important for each musician to claim ownership of the process and to view this as additive, not as taking anything away. "If this solution is to work, it must be something you all embrace, not with a sense of giving something up but with the knowledge that you need to work together and grow with and toward each other," says the coach.

Isabel, the second violinist, comes up with the next invention. "How about if I transpose the cello part and play that for a while? We can all take on the part of another and see how if feels to play the other's role," she explains.

Here Rachel joins in, saying she had been quite moved to hear Arthur expressing a sense of insecurity during the reframing discussion. "I feel the same way," she says. "At times I feel like a second fiddle, so to speak. I would love to listen to your solos critically while sincerely assuring you that I am here to offer helpful suggestions and not to judge your ability. I would ask for the same approach from you."

Two members of the group think these ideas would be very difficult to carry through on their own. Arthur suggests that another invention might be to have regular sessions with the coach, since an independent observer has seemed so helpful in these discussions.

A new sense of adventure and creative exploration infuses the group. But there is also a certain wariness that keeps the players on edge and anxious about whether these good ideas will be sustained and implemented.

5

Action

Setting Joint Agendas

Conventional negotiation often fails to ameliorate intransigent conflict, partly because procedure is too often placed before content in negotiation planning. There is a misdirected confidence that if only parties can be brought to the table, by promises and threats if necessary, the momentum of mere contact and the victory of rationality will work wonders.[1] Joint decisions about the substance and sequence of a negotiating agenda are regularly left until the start of formal talks. This is a primary reason talks often stall, particularly when conflicts are deeply rooted in identity issues.

Ensuring full and solid substantive preparation greatly enhances the odds of satisfactory agreement. Again, this is especially true when conflicts are identity-based, regardless of whether parties are involved in formal negotiation, program development, problem solving, or designing confidence-building initiatives. The first three phases of the ARIA framework may contribute to fostering effective substantive preparation. They can help provide clarity and agreement about what is essential to address.

After such agreement is crafted, through conceptual reframing of problems and invention of creative solutions, comes setting the agenda for the implementation of ideas. Most important, this fourth phase of ARIA should be from the start an intensively collaborative process. This is contrary to common notions of agenda setting as a competitive process in which disputants jockey to gain advantage over each other at the starting line. Indeed, it is commonly accepted that those who set the agenda reap the most benefits.[2] Instead, if both sides are setting the agenda cooperatively, it stands to reason that both sides and their interdependent needs and interests will be the beneficiaries.

In traditional preparations for negotiation, detailed agenda-setting and action-planning discussions are usually left until the start of formal talks. This may work fine when parties share many common concerns and goals. In deep conflict, however, this can lead to the end of a negotiation or problem-solving process before it can really begin. Substantive agreements about what is on and off the table, and in what order issues will be addressed should, if possible, be reached during the preparatory phases when a cooperative momentum is being fostered (Gross-Stein, 1989). If this is done, the likely success of the next steps, such as beginning formal negotiations, developing programs, and solving problems, improves significantly (Rothman, 1991).

Even if the final stages of resolving identity conflicts are arduous, as they frequently are, if they are built upon a foundation of cooperation, a positive momentum can be maintained into a solution-implementation phase. A mutual understanding about the nature and parameters of the conflict and how best to address them is crucial. If this cooperative spirit is in place, the parties can devote their energy to coordinating substantive discussions instead of competing for advantage. In an apt description, a former diplomat suggested that peace would benefit from a focus on substance, not procedures. "Instead of investing expensive political capital in unproductive diplomatic wrangling to convene preliminary talks on procedural steps for the discussion of modality . . . designed to lead to negotiations on provisional arrangements, the parties and powers—and, in particular, peace—would be much better served by a major effort on their part to tackle directly the core issues of the conflict" (Rafael, 1990, p. 4).

Addressing the core substantive issues in preparatory phases also helps deal with another major stumbling block to initiating formal negotiations or other forms of problem solving—the question of who should be at the table. In the U.S.-Vietnamese peace talks, procedural wrangling over the shape of the table was really about who would be present at the negotiations representing which issues and with what degree of authority. If negotiators could deeply understand the specific context and motivations surrounding the other side's core concerns, which are usually—and wrongheadedly—kept hidden and obscure, the road to mutual gains would be paved.

The action-planning phase serves to apply earlier substantive insight through a kind of recapitulation and joint assessment of goals, needs, and motivations. A move toward implementation also requires a reexamination of preliminary, provisional inventions. The procedures for setting the agenda can be broken down into stages that answer the following simple questions:

What is to be done?

Why is it to be done?

Who is to do it?

How is it to be done?

If these questions sound familiar, it is because they are similar to those asked during reflexive reframing. The difference lies in the focus; in the reframing phase the frame is only conceptual whereas here, as with inventing, the focus is practical.

Researchers and practitioners alike agree that "effective planning and preparation [are] the most critical elements in achieving negotiation objectives" (Lewicki and Litterer, 1985, p. 45). Moreover, having some kind of agreed-upon procedure for arriving at joint decisions about issues and the order of discussion is essential. What follows is a simple procedural framework to guide agenda setting and action planning.

Ready, Set the Agenda

When moving from invention into implementation, the first question the parties must address cooperatively goes something like this: In order to build upon our reflexive insights about the shared nature of our problems and to implement the inventions we have generated to cooperatively address them, what is the most useful level, scale, and type of action to pursue? This is an important strategic question that will be answered differently in every situation. However, it is possible to spell out some variables that parties may choose from to help guide them in this process. In cooperatively designing an agenda to consolidate and implement previous agreements and substantive breakthroughs, it is constructive for disputants to first decide on the scale and level of their initial actions. Some options (of increasing complexity) include designing an agenda for the following:

- Project planning around specific inventions

- Institution building to develop a mechanism to coordinate and implement a number of inventions sequentially or simultaneously

- Formal problem solving or negotiation, which constitutes the highest level of complexity and political action

The first two levels can either stand alone or become building blocks to the third. Another design might see formal negotiation supported by simultaneous processes being conducted at lower levels. Yet another way proceeds directly to formal negotiation but suspends the process temporarily if participants get stuck. Work then shifts to the lower levels to focus on generating new creativity or confidence.

Project Planning

There are benefits to designing the first step so that confidence in cooperation is fostered in a tangible, incremental way. Specific initiatives can be tackled first, zeroing in on inventions that are big enough to matter but small enough to work. As one example, initial energy could be usefully channeled into a cooperative, educational coexistence program. This is important but relatively noncontroversial and can be generalized across all sides. Such a program can stand alone as valuable in intergroup peace building and can also be viewed as a necessary piece of the overall puzzle of cooperation.

People in many urban neighborhoods in America and elsewhere live with ongoing racial tension. Usually such tension simmers quietly under the surface, but occasionally it flares into open hostility and violence. These communities often consist of people with different ethnic backgrounds and cultures. Small-scale actions such as those undertaken in project planning can go a long way toward alleviating conflict in such neighborhoods. One example might be to plan a playground for the community. This may seem like a small thing, but being tied to the reflexive process makes it larger. Residents would not just be building a playground, they would be doing something that promotes the possibility of dignity, mutual respect, and equality, both symbolically and practically in the deliberation, design, and construction of the playground.

Institution Building

In some cases, however, it may make more sense to launch right into developing some kind of coordinating apparatus or institutional structure. Given the complexity of the problem and interconnected nature of the various proposed solutions, an institutional framework may be necessary to implement a number of inventions in an integrated and systematic way. One example would be to set up a coordinating body or intercommunal conflict management institution that can implement solutions in several areas (education and joint recreational activities, for example) simultaneously.

In many communities across America, volunteer organizations are established to bring together various community actors to address community problems. In one community in New Hampshire, citizens fought bitterly over a previous and disastrous legacy of low-income housing and what future arrangements should or should not be made for providing affordable housing. A local community organization, "Dialogue for Decisions," brought together local activists and community leaders for deliberation and rational discussion.

Negotiation or Problem Solving

A third option is to dive right into a politically ambitious effort to consolidate and deepen the range of inventions through a formal problem-solving or negotiation process. One could argue that confidence has already been generated during preceding phases and that given the highly politicized nature of the problems, it is best to hasten right to more formal proceedings. Viewing the work that has come before as a form of prenegotiation, the insights that arose during the framing and inventing phases may be marshaled to promote a cooperative and ultimately successful formal process of problem solving or negotiation.

A New Hampshire community had to arrive at decisions about how to use federal monies for subsidized and affordable housing. Given their previous negative experiences with low-income housing in the community, many local leaders and citizens were opposed to having any program at all. Eventually, through a fairly cooperative process, agreements were negotiated for developing new, affordable housing, though the number of units initially sought was reduced. The community came up with a solution that would not stigmatize those living in the housing and that prevented large concentrations of the housing units by dispersing them throughout the town. Through the process a new community spirit of unity and a sense of local empowerment evolved.

There are advantages and disadvantages of each starting place, be it project initiation, institution building, or formal negotiation. Different decisions will be appropriate for different conflicts, given the specific set of factors, timing, and context. For instance, if the various constituents are highly suspicious of each other, then going slow to go fast and gradually constructing pieces of peace may well be the most prudent beginning. All sides can tackle one initiative at a time until some critical mass of confidence and success has been achieved.

Conversely, progressing in gradual steps can backfire if some of the participants are particularly impatient. It can also be a problem if moving incrementally would be viewed as a form of "false consciousness," whereby the underdogs are to be mollified to stop them from militating for deep and lasting changes. In that case an overarching political process is still premature, given the level of mutual suspicion and attributions of evil intentions that may still be prevalent in a protracted conflict. A more systemic process of weaving together a number of initiatives simultaneously under some kind of joint institutional umbrella may well be more functional and fruitful. Therefore, in many cases the process of preparing for negotiation is best achieved by pursuing small initiatives or weaving together a number of them.

At some point—at a certain date perhaps—the disputants will undoubtedly feel, "Enough with the piecemeal action. Let the real show begin." Still, the most important thing to keep in mind before disputants arrive at this point is that the preparatory work should be portrayed as an essential part of the total package of peace. Participants should not view the prior stages as only what happened "before" but as part and parcel of what must happen "after." Here a useful metaphor to keep in mind is the holographic model in which a whole picture is constituted of minipictures of that whole (Morgan and Ramirez, 1984).

Action Planning

Regardless of the scale of the first concrete steps taken, the following design questions must be answered to move from ideas to implementation: What outcomes are sought? Why? By whom? How?

Goals and Outcomes (What?)

The first step in the action-planning phase is to restate the problem in terms of the tasks to be accomplished. This step recapitulates the outcome of reflexive reframing in terms of common problems and a shared understanding of the nature of the conflict. Moreover this is important to ensure that parties are working on the same task and attempting to solve the same problem, which is essential to an effective and cooperative process. There are often many components of a conflict. Similarly, different parties emphasize different components at different times, given their own concerns and priorities. By agreeing to a task statement (derived from a joint frame about a conflict and its nature), parties are starting off in step.

It is useful to determine what should be on the table and in what order before decisions about specific participants are made. It should be clear that who should participate in what action is most constructively determined in response to specific decisions about what is to be done. Setting the order of the agenda is another delicate and important matter. Decisions about the content of the agenda and its order are potential minefields best discussed openly while setting an action agenda. Whether the end decision is to put easy, hard, or confidence-building issues first may be less important than the fact that all parties arrive at this decision together. Such agreements, if reached, can provide significant momentum for moving into more substantial problem solving. Instead of competing for advantage, parties instead are able to devote their energies to coordinating an agenda for substantive discussions.

Motives (Why?)

Next, in order to place objectives, desired outcomes, and the deep motivations at stake at the forefront of the process, it is useful to return to a discussion about which needs and values the sides want to satisfy in completing the tasks. Such a review can significantly contribute to keeping the parties moving forward. For example union and management leaders, having agreed to prepare for cooperative negotiations, should spell out the respective needs and values (dignity, recognition, participation, for example) they believe can be met best through such a process. This is important for gaining credibility from their respective constituencies and for keeping everyone focused.

Participants (Who?)

All too often the process of determining who the participants should be is a loaded political issue instead of a practical and functional determination. By placing content before process and articulating clearly what topics are to be covered and in what order, who should be at the table should be somewhat self-evident. In a number of protracted ethnic conflicts—in Sri Lanka, in the Middle East, in South Africa, and in Northern Ireland—a place at the table for liberation movement leaders (viewed by those in power as terrorists) has been one of the most politicized of decisions. When possible, if these politicized decisions can be made more functional—Who must be at the table to deliver a solution?—barriers to effective negotiation are greatly reduced. (This is what happened with the entry of the African National Congress and the Palestinian Liberation Organization into political negotiations with their former adversaries.) Thus agreements about what is on the agenda can lead to subsequent decisions about who is most likely to make an agreement that can be implemented. As much as possible, interlocutors should be determined by their attributes, such as technical expertise, political influence, and legitimacy, as well as prior experience.

Modalities (How?)

Recalling that one of the purposes of the agenda-setting phase is to place content before process, only now in the planning stage are parties encouraged to be specific about which modalities they plan to use in addressing their problems. (Sometimes this phase must precede the previous one, with decisions about who should be at the table being finalized only after determinations of how peace will progress have been made.) Whenever it occurs, this phase is used to make decisions about the process of subsequent joint activities.

In considering modalities, it is important to think about obstacles that will be confronted and ways to overcome them. Planning in advance how to handle both restraining and driving forces greatly improves the chances of success. Ideally, all sides will agree to act cooperatively (helping the other side sell agreements to those who would resist them, for example) and proactively (perhaps by enlisting the media and public opinion to further forward movement).

In an example from a labor negotiation, both union and management representatives might announce to their respective constituencies that they plan to hold company-wide discussion groups six months prior to formal negotiations. They can point out that this will allow both management and workers to develop a shared vision for a negotiating process that will be cooperative and produce mutually beneficial outcomes. In doing so, they would do well to think through how to present their plan in order to gain the early involvement of those who have previously found comfort and even meaning in perpetuating adversarial relations. Moreover, they might identify others who have apparently been dissatisfied with the status quo and encourage them to take on informal leadership roles.

Conclusion

Participants in a conflict resolution process may feel a let-down when the process draws near its conclusion and settles into the action-planning phase. The more technical phase of taking care of business at the end can feel anticlimactic after the earlier dynamism of reflexivity and the creativity of inventing. The sense of energy and discovery wanes, and now the seemingly small details are left. However, these details are crucial because they carry the process into action. This is where the philosophical and relatively abstract talk of reflexivity and resonance comes down to earth. And although not quite so emotional, it is still powerful when people begin to see that their efforts will have practical consequences.

The concrete solutions of the action-planning stage may sometimes seem small—organizing an employee appreciation day or forming a joint union-management committee. In fact, it may seem like these actions would have been possible without the process that came before; someone from "on high" could easily have ordained a committee or an appreciation day. But if that had been the case, the actions would have been artificially imposed and not directly tied to the underlying needs and values that were surfaced as the core of the conflict. The actions are powerful because they address what were earlier determined by parties in the conflict to be their essential concerns. The process of action planning, and even inventing to some extent, is instrumental and technical but also rooted in the fundamental needs and values that have been expressed within and between the disputing groups. This can sustain the powerful momentum that has been established.

One of the jobs of the facilitator or the mediator is to refocus attention on what is at stake in the conflict. Core concerns may easily be forgotten by participants when everyone is concentrating on working out details. The facilitator needs to help the parties recall the deep issues that must be addressed in any solution. The planning of action should serve to build confidence and foster the creative momentum, thus allowing everyone involved to sense that they are translating relatively abstract discourse about needs and values into meaningful aspects of the everyday functional affairs of people's lives and relationships.

The ARIA Quartet: Action

In approaching the final phase of action planning, the coach suggests that it would be helpful to ask four fairly simple questions:

What is to be done? Why is it to be done? Who is to do it? How is it to be done?

What Is to Be Done?

By this time it is becoming clear what needs to be done. Isabel speaks for the group. "We need to take advantage of our differences as a way to create a better working dynamic during rehearsals," she says. "As it is now, we're closing down and turning away from each other. Instead we must find a way to use our differences as an opportunity for growth and synergy. If we can do that, I know that we can really make this music soar." The coach suggests that one way to accomplish that goal is to pay close attention when old ways start to recur. "You must catch yourselves when you regress and be your own coaches," he warns. "Go out into the audience with your mind's eye and observe what is happening; strive to stop undermining each other due to your differences. Seek instead to be proactive and employ your diversity for resonance."

Why Is It to Be Done?

"I can say why it has to be done," says Rachel, the cellist. "Because I think we all know we're good, maybe even on the edge of greatness. But we're not there yet. There's some really hard work ahead, but the payoff could be enormous."

"Exactly!" exclaims the coach. "And you can use this conflict, the dynamism of your differences, to help you over hurdles and guide you on your way to excellence, to true harmony within your group and the music you create together."

Who Is to Do It?

The group agrees that they all need to participate in this process. "I feel like I'll be more able to stop myself now and observe my feelings when I'm getting frustrated. I can better direct my responses," offers Arthur. "Or at least," says Anthony, "I think perhaps we can each be willing to voice our disagreements and concerns with more confidence that the others won't jump on us or close down when we say what we are feeling."

"And if we need some feedback, we should be able to expect it in a way that won't make us defensive," says Isabel.

Arthur reiterates his belief that the coach needs to be involved on an ongoing basis. "Yes," replies the coach, "if you feel you are in a moment of crisis, or if an opportunity is going to be missed due to an escalating conflict, that should be your signal to give me a call. However, the sooner you can become your own coaches, individually and as a group, the better."

And the coach has another idea. "When you ask, 'Who is to do it?' make the audience your 'who.' Watch your audience as you perform in this upcoming concert and feel what happens there," he says. "The audience can be your litmus test of whether your efforts are working."

He also suggests listening together to other recordings of the Brahms quartet and critiquing them to share perceptions about the interpretations of other musicians. "Next, critique your critique so even this process is increasingly self-conscious."

Rachel takes this idea even further. "I guess Mr. Brahms can be a 'who' too," she says. "We need to talk to him to see what he thinks about what we're doing."

The coach agrees that there can be quite broad notions about who needs to be involved but reiterates that the process has to start with all the individual members of the quartet.

How Is It to Be Done?

The conversation now shifts to how to accomplish their goals. One member suggests planning a new project such as a concert tour. Others think that is moving too fast and would prefer to grow more comfortable with their new approach.

The coach suggests that they might still need to make accommodations about how to run their rehearsals. "Not everything can be integrative," he says. "Sometimes some of you may feel you want to spend more time with a particular piece than others do, so you will need to learn be flexible. Once you have fostered an integrative spirit, using compromise from time to time is no sin."

"I guess the first thing we need to do is start being honest with each other," says Anthony. "We need to say what we mean and do what we say."

"Absolutely," agrees the coach. "The secret is not to avoid but to engage. And you will see the payoff if you can use this conflict as an opportunity for creativity. You need to commit to harmony in your quartet as well as in your music. But that also means accepting the fact that harmony sometimes comes from friction and resistance. After all, what is a musical note but the friction of a bow being drawn over a string?"

Quartet Coda (Conclusion)

Real change takes time. Despite the quartet's renewed enthusiasm and commitment, their next concert several weeks later is something of a disappointment. Each member feels very self-conscious, viewing the performance as stiff because they are watching themselves so closely. The reception from the audience is lukewarm. They call in the coach, who once again takes a tough stance. He asks, "What happened? Why was the concert not fully satisfying?"

Several members start to blame the others, at which point they all burst into laughter. The coach offers a reminder, "You see you are not quite past blaming others yet!"

"But at least now we know when we are doing it!" responds Isabel.

"You need to know that you are all on the same page and that your music will resonate only when you do, within each of you and between all of you and your audiences."

The ARIA quartet is currently in rehearsal for an upcoming concert.

Part II

The ARIA Framework in Practice

. . . .

Prenegotiation in Nations

Peace Building in Jerusalem

It is ironic that negotiation can make conflicts worse. Premature problem solving or negotiation can force conflicting parties to compromise without any firm basis for doing so. In premature negotiation, disputants may try to do the impossible—forge a feeling of mutuality out of hatred. Nowhere is this more true than in the long-standing conflict between the Israelis and the Palestinians.

In confronting this bitter, intractable conflict, *prenegotiation* is needed to prepare the ground for more formal negotiations to follow. The necessity for a confidence-building approach was highlighted at the conclusion of the historic Middle East Peace Conference held in Madrid in November of 1991, when the U.S. secretary of state, James Baker, spoke about the need for something more than formal negotiation in the peace process:

> The unwillingness of the parties to take confidence-building steps has been disappointing. You have dealt successfully with formulas and positions. You have agreed on terms of reference that are fair and equitable. You have launched a process of negotiations that can succeed. But you have failed to deal adequately with the human dimension of the conflict. . . . Formulas, terms of reference, and negotiations are not enough. Support for a negotiating process will not be sustained unless the

human dimension is addressed by all parties. A way must be found to send signals of peace and reconciliation that affect the peoples of the region (Baker, 1991, p. 809).

The Jerusalem Peace Initiative (part of the larger Program on Managing Political Disputes), which I directed from 1992 through 1994, was designed to emphasize and help address the human dimension of the Israeli-Palestinian conflict over Jerusalem. Sponsored by the Leonard Davis Institute for International Relations at the Hebrew University of Jerusalem, the Jerusalem Peace Initiative conducted dozens of conflict resolution, dialogue, and training workshops between Israelis and Palestinians and for various groups of students, community leaders and activists, policy makers, professional groups, and diplomats. In this chapter I will illustrate each phase of the ARIA method as a vehicle for prenegotiation by presenting real examples drawn from workshops that I conducted along with Palestinian cofacilitators between Israelis and Palestinians over the future of Jerusalem.[1]

I. Antagonism

In each workshop we (myself and a Palestinian cofacilitator) begin by asking both sides to present their positions on the future of Jerusalem, including how they define the problem and what solutions they might suggest. The participants then naturally recite their adversarial positions, defining the problem from their perspective and summarizing their preferred outcomes. As I previously discussed, such positional framing is usually sustained and deepened by blame, polarizing between Us and Them, attributing negative dispositions to the other side, and projecting. In the prototypical conflict-framing discussion to follow, each side paints the other as the problem, and each sets the stage for seeking solutions that are unacceptable to the other side. Thus division is deepened and antagonism rigidified.

Both sides are eager to jump in with their view of the problem. The Palestinians say Israel has illegally annexed Jerusalem as its own, denying the Palestinian people their legitimate right to self-determination in their own homeland. "Jerusalem is the core of our national struggle and must become the capital of our state," declares one participant. "We do not now and never will accept Israeli hegemony in this city." The Palestinians point out that Israelis have been making them feel vulnerable and despised by encircling neighborhoods in Jerusalem that the Palestinians feel are historically central to their national and religious life. "Israelis will claim that we have full and safe access to our holy sites, particularly our Al Aqsa Mosque, one of the most holy sites of Islam, but we must go there under their watch, and there we have been the recipients of their hatred and violence numerous times."

The situation is also clear-cut for the Israelis. "The problem over Jerusalem is simply that our legitimate rights and rule are not recognized." They point out that when Jerusalem was under Jordanian rule, holy sites were off-limits to them until they were attacked in 1967 and then liberated Jerusalem in response to the aggression. The Israelis say that now Jews, Moslems, and Christians alike have free and, for the most part, safe access to their respective holy places. They declare that Jerusalem has been and remains the focal point of the Jewish people and their religion, the historic capital of the Jewish nation as well as the vibrant national heartbeat of modern Israel. They feel beset upon by the Palestinians and those in the Arab world who claim Israelis have usurped Jerusalem. "We must stand strong. If we lose Jerusalem, Zionism will be doomed and Jews will once again be a scattered and defenseless people."

At this point we ask both sides how they view the other side around this issue. The Israelis accuse the Palestinians of being an aggressive and violent people who sustain themselves with a fantasy of an unrealistic future. They contend that since 1967 Israel has offered the Palestinians a hand in running the city by giving them democratic rights to vote and to run for office. They think it is hypocritical that Palestinians blame Israelis for not addressing their local interests when they refuse to participate in municipal governance, claiming not to accept Israeli sovereignty. They point out that Israel has given the Palestinian religious council, the *Wakf*, autonomous control over their holy sites. "But what do they do?" cries one Israeli. "Several times in recent years during our holiday of Sukkot, when Jews from all over Israel gather at the Wailing Wall recalling times when we prayed at our temple that stood on this spot, they throw stones down onto our heads from the Temple Mount where their Mosque now sits, as we pray at our Wall—the last remnant of our Temple. Then they cry to the world when our security forces act to defend us."

"Defend you!" interrupts a Palestinian. "By opening fire in retaliation for stones and killing many of our worshipers in cold blood! This is exactly the point. We cannot live under Israeli control for one day longer." This participant goes on to say that Israelis justify their suppression, violence, and injustice by claiming "security needs." "They have spilled our blood and repressed us as a kind of recompense for what others in other lands, like the Nazis, have done to them. We did not cause their suffering, but we suffer from it." An Israeli retorts, "What the Nazis failed to do, you are trying to finish."

Having heard the articulation of the deep antagonism between them, we step back to more objective issues and ask the participants to briefly describe what limited resources are at stake, since these are the tangible issues around which parties link their antagonism. (We seek to get this frame articulated and out in the open so it can later be observed and contrasted with a different identity-based analysis of their problems. It is around such concrete interests that antagonism is normally expressed and perpetuated. We will soon help parties reframe away from competition over resources to identifying the common needs and values underlying those resources.) The Israelis respond, "Territory, political control, or simply, sovereignty. We can't both be sovereign of the same spot." The Palestinians concur about the limited resources but say they believe those resources can be divided.

To conclude we ask that they summarize their positions in terms of outcomes they seek in any negotiation on the future of Jerusalem. This builds on the common adversarial conflict frame and antici-pates the kind of antagonistic negotiation process that would nor-mally follow. For the Palestinians this is simple—East Jerusalem must be the capital of their state. "First Gaza, then the West Bank, then Jerusalem, then all of what they call Palestine," respond the Israelis. "Autonomy will work perhaps, not only in the territories but even in Jerusalem, but nothing more. We will not withdraw one inch from Jerusalem."

In an ARIA workshop, we bring adversarial framing to a close by pointing out that the opposing sides have just repeated what they have always done. We ask them to take note of their antagonistic feelings and the relatively fruitless, though all too familiar, process we just revisited. Then we insist that what has just transpired is exactly what we seek to avoid from this point forward.

II. Resonance

In preparation for the reflexive discussion to follow, we surface the human dimension beneath both sides' antagonistic positions.

Laying the Groundwork for Understanding

As we seek to build a deep level of disclosure of what participants care about, we ask participants to introduce themselves in terms of their personal connection to Jerusalem, and we hear overlapping stories that illustrate their deep and emotional connections with the city.

Some offer personal histories combined with history of the city. "The history of my personal childhood . . . was being kept from the Old City," says one. "I am a true Jerusalemite," says another. "My family has lived here for fourteen centuries." Others express their fear to enter the other side of Jerusalem. "I don't feel safe or accepted on 'their' side. I feel barriers, hatred, and fear." But there is also hope for peace in the city. "While I would very much like to know the other side, it seems very far away." On the whole people express a wide range of personal, spiritual, and emotional attachments to the city. The introductions set a new tone for a real encounter between the participants.

In sharing thoughts and feelings on Jerusalem, the participants articulate their personal frames. Benjamin, a soldier in the Israeli army in 1967, expresses frustration that the hope both sides felt in 1967 that the fighting would end has gone unrealized. "I was born in Jerusalem, so I have always dealt with the dispute. When I was growing up the Jordanians forbade Jews to visit the Temple Mount and the Wailing Wall," recalls Benjamin. "I am aware that I cannot deport the Arabs, and I hope they understand they cannot exile me. I still have hope that we will find a way of living together without harming each other," he says. But his optimism is shaded by serious doubts about a political solution acceptable to both sides ever being found.

One participant, a Palestinian refugee named Osman, recounts a painful experience for him in 1991 during the Gulf War, in which Iraq launched Scud missile attacks against Israel. Osman explains that because his wife had a Jerusalem identity card they were able to register their first child, but not their second. "During the war, my second son, who was five years old at this time, said to me, 'You don't love me. You gave my brother a gas mask (to which he was 'entitled' as a Jerusalem resident), and I didn't get one. I'm afraid I am going to die.' When it comes to Jerusalem," Osman says, "we Palestinians are qualified to determine what we need because we have suffered. We are all graduates of the college of suffering."

Interactive Introspection

Following the introductions, participants begin to articulate their reflexive definitions of the conflict and what motivates it, from the inside out. We ask them to describe how Jerusalem is core to the hopes and fears of their people and to the conflict as a whole.

The Palestinians begin by insisting that Al Quds (Jerusalem) is the center from which their national, cultural, and religious lives emanate. Saying that all Arabs are justified in claiming the city as their birthright, one participant says, "For us Palestinians our link with Jerusalem is equal to our own sense of national selfhood." He also asserts that Jerusalem has always been the main nerve of Palestinian intellectual and economic life. "Without Jerusalem, we will remain what we have become—a fragmented, poorly led, somewhat unfocused collection of tribes," he concludes. "With Jerusalem, our national unity is assured."

The Israelis say that Jerusalem and the Jewish people are synonymous, always have been and always will be. "Jerusalem is the key to our continuity," one says. "For the past three thousand years our ancestors either lived here or prayed daily to live here. We must pass it on to future generations as a birthright, for only thus will we as a people, a culture, a religion, and a nation ensure our own future." Another responds that if Israel loses hold of Jerusalem politically, "it would only be a matter of time before we lose hold of the rest of Israel stage after stage."

At this point the workshop facilitators acknowledge that the hopes and fears both sides express are very powerful and moving to us, and we assume to the participants as well (thus modeling a process of openness, active listening, and self-disclosure we hope to encourage). We seek to build upon the new mood emerging around the table by accenting the new introspective and emotional frames just voiced. We briefly summarize their deep concerns and ask them to say more about the hopes, values, and needs that are at stake for them personally; we ask them to speak also as representatives of their broader communities. Interactive introspection grows. An Israeli says, "We need Jerusalem [in order] to be who we are and who we will become; it is equivalent to our identity. It gives us cultural, religious, national, and political meaning and purpose. This may sound a little grandiose, but we need Jerusalem [if we are] to continue to be bigger than our size. We are small, but Jerusalem helps to make us larger."

The Palestinian side is equally passionate and personal. "Our history has been marked by occupations by foreigners. We aspire to control our own destiny; this is only really possible with Jerusalem as our religious and political core. With Jerusalem, we will gain the internal political and national cohesion and the external recognition that we lack and require."

Now we ask the participants to ask each other questions for clarification. We stress that they should not engage in a typical positional debate, which we have already experienced during the adversarial framing at the beginning of the workshop. We urge them to try to take the word of the other side that these are their perceptions and that they do believe they have these needs, even if some doubt the accuracy of the other side's perceptions or that they really require fulfillment of the needs they assert. "Ask questions so that you may attempt to understand them and their values and needs, as they themselves perceive them, even if you don't agree with them," we suggest. "Only through deeply understanding what motivates the other side and their perceptions about their reality will you gain the insights needed to work with them, not against them, and to solve the conflict together."

It does not take long before we must intervene to redirect the discussion. An Israeli begins the conversation with this statement: "You say Jerusalem is your unity, but this is only a new . . . "

We stop him there, pointing out that it sounds as if he is about to score a point, as one does in a positional debate. "Here we want questions for clarification, understanding, and analytic empathy," we say. "You need not agree with their perceptions, but at least try to understand them." To further emphasize this point, we tell them that soon we may be asking them to role play the other side to test out whether they have gained sufficient analytic empathy to move forward in the process. With that in mind, we urge them to use this time to gather information and insight to prepare for that. "Ask in a way that encourages them to answer so that you can learn something you didn't know," we say.

The Israeli starts over with a question: "Why has Jerusalem become so important to you in terms of Palestinian peoplehood? This is a relatively new concern for you. Less than a hundred years ago you cared about it only religiously; now you say it is your national core. Why?"

A Palestinian agrees that their national consciousness is a relatively recent phenomenon. "Still it is undeniable that it motivates everything we think and do religiously, historically, culturally, and politically. I should think that you, of all people, should be able to understand this spiritual and political connection we have with Jerusalem!"

Another Palestinian asks why the Israelis need to rule over them. We break in to ask him to phrase his question a little less provocatively. We explain that we are seeking to promote active listening for understanding, which requires both an openness to hear what the other side has to say about itself and also a willingness to ask questions so that the other side wants to answer honestly and nondefensively. He agrees to try. "If your safety and access to your holy sites and the Jewish areas were assured, wouldn't it be a relief not to rule over Palestinians in East Jerusalem who are hostile to you?"

The Israeli sees this situation as too hypothetical. "Our security has never been assured and will only be secured by our own efforts. We can never again entrust our destiny to others—and certainly not to others who have at one time vowed to destroy us."

The reflexive dialogue continues in this vein, with questions, clarification, silence, and understanding. It is not a short process; it can take several days. But finally we reach a point when we test each side's analytic empathy by asking participants to articulate the other side's deepest concerns in a mini role reversal. This effort proves so successful that at the end one Israeli jokingly says to the Palestinians, "Why don't you represent our interests at the U.N.?"

The Meshing of Needs

Having moved from the articulation of each voice to recognition of those voices, we feel the two sides can now move forward and seek to build some resonance. "You have both spoken about how deeply your own histories and futures are wrapped up in Jerusalem," we say. "How might your separate voices together create a single song?"

An Israeli politician speaks up first. "For forty-five years I have been working for how we can live together in a different Jerusalem," he says. "I don't want my children to live through what I lived through. I believe you feel the same. I don't want my son to have to fight and see his friends and relatives get killed defending the city. I'm determined that my children and your children live together in this city in a way that fulfills its namesake as a city of peace."

Now a Palestinian speaks. "I'm determined that my son and daughters not face the indignity of feeling smaller than any other people. I'm determined that my children will have a dignified life in this most dignified of all cities. And so I too am determined that together we create a city where Palestinians and Israelis can both live unafraid and with pride."

An Israeli responds that in light of their discussions it is clear that any future for Jerusalem can only be formed by including the Palestinians, not in opposition to them. "We understand that our new history includes you, and will only be achieved in a way that is whole if it continues to include you. Jerusalem is a place that links us each with our people in powerful ways, and if we can work with each other, together we might create a Jerusalem that is for all people."

It is always a powerful moment when, often for the first time, both sides feel that their adversary has truly heard them. When parties can share this process of interactive reflection, a new foundation can be built. In this case the groundwork is laid by defining both sides' needs, goals, and values that are frustrated and threatened in this ongoing conflict. By listening closely to the needs and fears of others, both sides can realize that the problem is no longer defined solely as whether Jerusalem will be a "unified" or a "divided" city. Instead the real question is how they will share the city in ways that neither feels are ultimately threatening to their identity needs.

III. Invention

The question of who owns Jerusalem is overwhelming and ultimately, if true peace is the goal, is the wrong question. The bigger questions, based on needs and identity, might be, How are we all going to be safe? How can everyone have control over their own destiny? How can we each gain full and unfettered expression of our identity without limiting that of the other side? And as the inventing process gets under way, those big questions are addressed by incremental and functional answers. It is important to focus on manageable solutions while inventing as many specific integrative ideas as possible. Although economic cooperation and enhanced cultural expression, for example, may seem like relatively small steps at first, they can nourish a great deal of momentum to address underlying needs and prepare the ground for political solutions, including compromise when necessary.

Thus as the process moves into the inventing stage, the participants brainstorm a number of possible approaches. They decide to focus on developing functional solutions and ideas related to local politics and municipal governance, economics, personal and communal safety, cultural expression, and education (see Rothman, Land, and Twite, 1994).

Principles Behind the Project

The participants believe that jointly defining shared problems and proposing mutually beneficial solutions can contribute to both the will-to-peace and confidence-in-peace that are so necessary to bring peace about. However, they recognize that they are addressing the question of designing functional solutions to daily problems in the absence of a mutually acceptable political solution. Participants need to feel confident that their involvement will in no way compromise the political positions they hold. To this end, the Israeli and Palestinian participants formulate the following statement of principle:

Opinions vary in this group regarding the future of
Jerusalem, the political status of which is still contested.
Some of us believe that a durable peace cannot be
achieved unless the problem is solved on the basis of
equality and justice that demands dividing or sharing
sovereignty and coordinating and/or separating municipal responsibilities over the city. Others believe that
Jerusalem should continue under the sovereign rule of
Israel but with extensive autonomy and self-rule afforded
to the Palestinians. Thus while we all believe significant
changes must occur, we are at odds with each other
about the shape and dimensions of these changes. We do
not expect this project will change such positions;
indeed, it is not designed to do so. On the contrary, we
are illustrating in our work together a key purpose of
conflict resolution. Despite the fact that we hold adversarial political positions among ourselves, we can
nonetheless find common ground and build commitment to and confidence in peace through the conviction that as Israelis and Palestinians fated to live
together in the city of Jerusalem, we must learn to do
so in a better fashion than we do at present. Our project is designed in a modest way to contribute to Israeli-
Palestinian co-existence in Jerusalem through concrete
policy proposals for cooperative change and development in five functional areas of daily concern to both
communities: security, economics, education, municipal services and governance, and cultural expression.

The Proposals

The participants decide to write policy papers in mixed communal
teams about how to cooperatively address these five functional areas
central to life in Jerusalem. Their proposals are deliberately designed
to promote pieces of peace and build confidence that cooperation

will be possible. The goal is to simultaneously address underlying identity concerns while tangibly addressing resource issues as a means to that end. The process utilizes the integrative problem-solving techniques of differentiation, expansion, and compensation discussed in Chapter Five. Some teams find that all three techniques are useful; others use the techniques less but are still able to be integrative in their inventions.

Proposal #1: Local Politics and Municipal Governance

Expansion: In their proposal the team suggests that the city of Jerusalem must be visualized as a focal point of historical attachment and national significance for both communities. They further suggest that a bi-communal city council be established, representing all interests and controlling services such as education, road development, water works, and health and welfare.

Differentiation: They suggest that within each community, power over issues such as social services, cultural activities, and local planning should be handed over to appropriate neighborhood authorities. Moreover, they feel that trust can be built between Israeli and Palestinian communities by establishing strong neighborhood institutions that will diffuse authority and give a degree of autonomy to all communities.

Proposal #2: Economics

Expansion: The team recommends the expansion of tourism through the establishment of a Joint Tourism Commission for the city, sponsored jointly by the Israeli Ministry of Tourism and the Palestinian Higher Council of Tourism. This bi-national commission could organize promotional activities, cooperatively manage key sites, organize training for the industry, and own and operate joint ventures. Moreover they state that business leaders from both communities should cooperate to attract investment from overseas for the city as a whole and in particular for joint ventures for which both could secure backing.

Differentiation: Participants agree that Palestinians have particular access to Arab markets in the Middle East and can provide a link and bridge for the city as a whole. Technical education should be improved, especially in the Eastern (Palestinian) part of the city. East Jerusalem has few technical schools or colleges, and this handicaps the Palestinians living there, preventing them from making their full contribution to the fiscal health of the city. Although construction is vigorous in West Jerusalem, for political reasons it has lagged in the East. This must be rectified and will provide an area for significant economic development.

Compensation: The team suggests that due to unequal development between the two communities, special efforts need to be made to raise the economic and educational level of the Palestinians. In exchange for this, Israelis will gain greater well-being both directly, by benefiting from Palestinian economic development, and indirectly, by living with neighbors who are not envious and resentful.

Proposal #3: Personal and Communal Safety

Expansion: This group concludes that a joint police force should be established in which Palestinians will serve alongside Israelis, with joint patrols to be organized in certain neighborhoods. The force will operate initially in the Old City and neighboring Palestinian areas. Joint training for police personnel from both communities will be organized. Provisions will be made for the establishment of a mediation center (employing both traditional Arab methods of "sulha" and western techniques), which will provide means of defusing local conflict by making available trained mediators to the parties in conflict. A crisis prevention hotline to the mediation center will be available to the police, community leaders, and the general public.

Proposal #4: Cultural Relations

This team is made up of an Israeli playwright and theater director and a Palestinian anthropologist and author. They find themselves cooperating to produce a play that is intended to demonstrate how culture can at once bring people together and illustrate in dramatic form some of the unresolved issues between the two communities in Jerusalem. (This play, called *The Jasmine Bush*, was performed in Jerusalem in 1995 in a mixture of English, Hebrew, and Arabic, with a mixed cast of Palestinian and Israeli actors, and to mixed audiences. It was the first play ever cowritten and coacted by Israelis and Palestinians, and it achieved much favorable, as well as controversial, public and media attention.)

Proposal #5: Education

The education team notes in its preamble that provisions for cooperation already exist in the stated aims of the Israeli and Palestinian school systems and should be vigorously encouraged. If implemented they will do much to improve relationships and mutual understanding. For example the stated aims of the Jordanian curriculum, which has been the basis for the Palestinian educational system for decades, include the desire "to foster the notions of peace, respect for human values, and understanding and cooperation on the basis of equality." (This Jordanian system will continue to underpin much of the educational system in the West Bank and Gaza, even under autonomy or independence.) The Israeli Ministry of Education has a special unit with no other purpose than to promote the idea of democracy and Arab-Jewish coexistence. (Since the peace process began, this unit has gained momentum and has dedicated itself to developing educational curriculum to teach about peace.)

Expansion: Besides activating existing guidelines, this team singles out as essential the allocation of resources to each community in Jerusalem in accordance with its needs on a fair and just basis. Other proposals include establishing a joint review committee made up of educators and scholars from both communities that would examine existing curricula and textbooks, with an eye toward improving the quality of materials and promoting mutual understanding. They also propose the establishment of a centralized framework within the city for promoting contacts between educators and students from the two communities. They conclude with the suggestion of joint extracurricular activities for school children of all ages, including field trips and athletic programs.

IV. Action

At the conclusion of the Jerusalem Peace Initiative Project, the mixed teams suggest specific confidence-building initiatives to address the policy proposals in education, security, municipal governance, culture, and economics. Building upon specific initiatives from each of the five teams, the project coordinators also propose an institutional "container" for them, as described shortly. Finally, to address the third type of action planning, negotiation, or problem solving, the chapter concludes with a discussion of a framework for negotiation that could be derived from the work of the Jerusalem Peace Initiative.

First, here is an illustration of a confidence-building initiative, one of the education team's proposals.

Project Planning

The education team proposes a simple design for implementing several of its key inventions:

Outcomes: Establish a joint committee for examining the textbooks of both sides. Make recommendations about missing material in the curricula of both sides that would help promote mutual understanding, tolerance, and coexistence.

Objectives: To eliminate prejudicial and stereotypical material from textbooks. Promote material that will enhance greater understanding and respect for the other side, as well as each side's national identity.

Participants: High-level educators, professionals, and respected community leaders from each side.

Modalities: Use an international advisory board to help the committee develop criteria for material to be included or excluded in textbooks. This board will also review minutes from the committee's regular meetings and will ultimately sponsor the development of new texts.

Institution Building

In consultation with the project's participants, the staff of the Jerusalem Peace Initiative drafted a proposal for the establishment of a bi-communal and nongovernmental Jerusalem Center for Conflict Resolution.[2] This Center, if established, would serve to coordinate and consolidate the various inventions proposed by the Jerusalem Peace Initiative, as well as many other sincere efforts to build a foundation for cooperation in the city.

Outcomes: In the name of the participants of the Jerusalem Peace Initiative, we propose the immediate establishment of the Jerusalem Center for Conflict Resolution. It has become clear to us as we wrap up our Jerusalem Peace Initiative that it will only reach practical fruition in the context of sustained and ongoing activities in the setting of a developed institutional framework. Moreover, it has become clear during the course of the project that many of those with whom we were in contact in relation to our work on Jerusalem shared our view that there was a need for such an institutional framework providing an ongoing opportunity for conflict resolution training, intervention, and activity.

Objectives: It is our hope that this idea will be carried forward and that it will provide more impetus for efforts to creatively address social conflicts of all kinds in this region. This is especially true in functional issues such as those addressed in our Jerusalem Peace Initiative: security issues; education and its positive socializing role in each respective society in promoting coexistence between both societies; cultural contacts and interaction; economic cooperation; and a fair and sensible approach to municipal government. There has been no sustained effort to date to train individuals from the various communities so that they can (either through working in the organizations or communities from which they come, or as mediators working from a recognized central institution) help reduce the impact of, or solve, conflicts at an international, national, or local level. Moreover, there is no existing institution or organization that can provide such training for mediators and that is recognized as being of practical value in preventing or reducing the negative impact of serious conflict. Therefore an institution is needed in which members of the different ethnic groups likely to be involved in conflict can work together and provide mediation between Israelis and Palestinians, Israeli Jews and Israeli Arabs, and within these communities as well.

Participants: A high-level and active local board (including public figures from a wide political spectrum from both communities), an international advisory board, joint directors (one Palestinian and one Israeli), and a small and communally mixed support staff. Conflict resolution training for staff and volunteer associates will be provided both by local experts and individuals from abroad who have special knowledge of the region and its conflicts.

Modalities: Such an institution should be highly analytic and self-reflective; it cannot however, be primarily academic. Instead it ought to be a model of self-reflective practice with a view toward influencing conceptions about conflict and its management through *empirical work and study, practices* (through training and conflict intervention), and *policy* (through engagement of high-level politicians and policy makers in the workings and results of the envisioned institution). It will operate along the following lines:

1. Provide training in conflict resolution for Israelis (both Arab and Jewish) and Palestinians. This training would have as its prime objective to equip those involved with the tools for practicing mediation in conflict situations and provide from

among the successful students of the training courses a body of skilled mediators from both major ethnic groups.

2. Gain acceptance from Israeli and Palestinian authorities who would see in it a vehicle for creatively addressing conflict— conflict that initially might seem small and controlled but could otherwise escalate and pose serious threats to peace.

3. Operate a higher-level hotline, which on request could send highly trained professional mediators to address particularly volatile conflicts.

4. Initiate and sustain bi-communal peace-making projects like the Jerusalem Peace Initiative.

Negotiation

If negotiation is about finding a middle ground between mutually exclusive positions, then Jerusalem presents a negotiator's ulti-mate challenge. There is broad agreement among most Israelis that Jerusalem must remain "united" under their sovereign con-trol, with differences of opinion regarding only how much auton-omy Palestinians ought to be ultimately granted. Conversely, Palestinians are fairly united in what they view as a minimal demand that they gain control over Eastern Jerusalem as the cap-ital of the state they seek to establish. These are the starting points in applying the ARIA framework to the Jerusalem conflict (Figure 6.1).

Building upon the reframing and inventing steps, a negotiation agenda should initially move away from attempting to find a mid-dle ground between these incompatible positions. Instead, the identity needs each position represents should be addressed through concrete and functional interests that might bridge the communities through a process of self-interested cooperation and positive interdependence.

The five areas addressed by the participants in the Jerusalem Peace Initiative—municipal governance, education, culture, safety,

Figure 6.1. Applying ARIA in the Jerusalem Conflict.

Antagonism

Unified rule under Israeli sovereignty   Divided rule with East Jerusalem as
capital of Palestinian State

Resonance

Safety
Dignity
Unity and Identity
Control
Well-being

↓

Invention

(Differentiation; Expansion; Compensation)

Municipal governance   Empower local neighborhoods.
Form bi-communal city council.

Economic development   Give Palestinians direct access to
Middle Eastern markets and
provide conduit for Israeli access.
Form joint tourism commission.
Raise economic standards of
Palestinian sector of city.

Security   Establish a mediation center;
set up joint police force; set up
crisis prevention hotline.

Cultural expression   Devise joint artistic creations (drama,
for example).

Education   Develop institutions and norms
that enhance spirit of tolerance
and cooperation.
Form joint curriculum review
committee.

↓

Action
(What? Why? Who? How?)

Confidence-building measures—such as a joint curriculum committee
Bridging institutions—such as a mediation center
Negotiation and Problem Solving—toward cooperative and integrative political
solutions

---

and economics—are good starting places for formal negotiation agendas as well. Building upon confidence generated in such areas, an agenda could be designed to negotiate ways to politically extend and consolidate gains in those functional areas. Negotiation would seek to bridge the positions of each side when possible (exploring, for example, how the boundaries of Jerusalem could be expanded, differentiated, or compensated such that neither side feels it must sacrifice core concerns) and, as negotiation must ultimately do, compromising as well (articulating what each side must give up in order to consolidate what it has gained).

Once a foundation of confidence has been established, negotiation committees could be created to explore more contentious issues in need of settlement. These might include such issues as land use and ownership, international recognition, institutions of state (embassies, economic institutions, and coordinating bodies), security arrangements, religious sites, and so forth. It might take many months, or even years, to reach agreements around these issues and to establish mechanisms to implement and monitor agreements. When that is accomplished, a supreme committee could be established to examine various political arrangements for Jerusalem and invent new and potentially integrative ones that could best satisfy the underlying identity needs of each community (such as enlarging the municipal boundaries of the city and thereby literally and symbolically expanding the range of options). At the same time, this committee could provide the most effective means of supporting and sustaining the kind of functional cooperation that will be proposed from each subcommittee.

The Jerusalem Peace Initiative took place at a time when the peace process between the Palestinians and the Israelis was stalled, and many saw the effort as futile. However, it is under just such divisive conditions that prenegotiation can be most useful. When formal negotiations are completely deadlocked, the work of peace can still proceed at the human and functional levels described in this chapter, thus laying the groundwork for renewed negotiations later.

In 1989, the acting assistant secretary of state for Near Eastern and South Asian affairs, Paul Hare, described prenegotiation as a process designed to overcome "gaps and suspicions . . . too deep to be bridged now by a formal initiative designed to launch negotiation. Rather . . . the efforts of all sides should be directed at narrowing gaps, overcoming suspicions, and establishing a climate that could sustain formal negotiations" (Hare, 1989, p. 9).

In many conflicts in which resource issues are not the primary cause (even when parties may initially think they are), and disputants lack shared tangible outcome goals, distributive negotiation procedures can be useful if they are preceded by integrative ones. In such a prenegotiation process disputants do not seek to reach binding agreements but rather to explore where cooperative, integrative efforts can help generate momentum and confidence that an eventual negotiation process, with all its give and take, will be mutually beneficial.

This kind of confidence building is precisely the first step that is required to help parties locked in intransigent conflict, in which existential issues loom so large, discover that cooperation with their adversaries can be the best and perhaps only way for them to fulfill their needs. Interdependent as they are, the needs of one side can often best be met, or only be met, through fulfillment of similar needs on the other side. After seeking for decades to either wholly disregard or destroy the other side, Israeli and Palestinian leaders are learning that they may best fulfill their respective needs for safety and survival through cooperation.

7

Transforming Conflicts Within and

Between Groups in Organizations

Given my professional background in the Middle East and the fact that in most of my public presentations the Jerusalem conflict provides the organizing metaphor for my work, participants in the conflict management work that I do with organizations and communities frequently approach me with the disclaimer, "We're not the Israelis and the Palestinians, but . . ." To some degree they can identify with the protractedness and the stress of bitter ethnic conflicts they read about in the papers. However, they assume that their conflict comes from different causes and has wholly different effects. Not necessarily. Many of the issues in ethnic conflicts, particularly threats and frustrations to core identity concerns, play a major role in our organizational and communal lives.

As in ethnic disputes, conflicts in organizational life frequently take place in two interlocking arenas: *within* teams at single levels of organization (between upper-management teams, for example) and *between* those teams and other teams (such as between management leaders and labor leaders). Resolving organizational conflicts requires that sets both *within* and *between* different groups be addressed interactively.

In this chapter I will explore the use and the principles of the ARIA framework in different arenas of organizational conflict. For ease of presentation I have merged several cases from my intervention work into one composite narrative—a drama, if you will—about a labor-management conflict in a fictitious hospital.

Within and Between

The setting is Mercy Medical Center, a 350-bed general service hospital in a midsize midwestern city. The hospital employs several hundred people; many are members of the Hospital Workers Union. The conflict is presented as a drama in three acts: Act One—transformation within union; Act Two—transformation within management; and Act Three—transformation between union and management.

The story begins on an intergroup level, as management and labor approach contract talks. However, the action quickly moves to intragroup conflicts within each side that must be addressed first, before progress between the two groups can be made and sustained. The two sides eventually do undertake an effort to work together to remedy a long history of intergroup conflict.

Act One: Transformation Within Union

> One problem that has been around for several decades and is ongoing involves relations between management and union. . . . This relationship is so mired in past history that extricating it from its crippling legacy of conflict seems impossible. . . . (Letter from Jen Jordan, vice president of administration and finance, Mercy Medical Center)

At the conclusion of a public lecture on my work in Israeli-Palestinian relations, I am approached by Jen Jordan, a vice president of Mercy Medical Center. She asks if what I had spoken about might be useful for the hospital's deeply conflicted labor-management relations. When I inquire how relations are within various levels of management, she looks at me quizzically and says "Fine" with a sheepish grin that reveals more than her verbal response.

The labor-management conflict at Mercy Medical has been going on for years—in fact, for decades. It is a system-wide conflict that fits the definition of an intransigent conflict: it is long-term, fluctuates in intensity, and threatens participants' sense of self, security, and efficacy; it is deeply embedded and resistant to significant efforts at negotiated solutions; and it is leading to low morale and a general sense of dissatisfaction. In one year the union and management will engage in their usual trauma of collective bargaining, a process many on both sides say they would love to change. They envision an atmosphere that would foster more productive and less acrimonious negotiations. Jen invites me to run seminars for union and management leaders on problem solving and consensus building between groups. My first assignment, however, is to get union leaders to sign up.

Scene One: The First Steps

I am willing to help, but I make it clear that I will be working for the entire system, including the union, even if management is picking up the tab. Given that the seminars are an initiative from management, and given the rancorous relations that have plagued management-union interactions for years, the union's motivation to participate is low. The first response from union leadership is that things are all right as they are. "It's not great, but then they never have been and we don't think they ever will be," says Carl, the local union president. "We think we probably are happy just to leave things as they are." In fact, it is clear that the union leaders (less so the general membership) perceive this idea as just another management ploy to gain control. Their organizing metaphor is that management is "a wolf in sheep's clothing."

One clear lesson I have learned in this work is that if motivation to engage in addressing conflicts is absent from the start, the whole process will be an uphill battle and probably fruitless. Clearly, getting disputants to want to engage in the first place is a crucial and essential job. Motivation cannot be forced, though sometimes it can be catalyzed.

Before throwing in the hat, I hold a few private discussions with individual union leaders to see if there might be any desire for dialogue expressed in private. There is. All express the idea that they are standing by the group's decision; however, several leaders deeply regret that the decision seems so final. "It certainly would be nice to communicate better with them," says one. "Please try," urges another. Several influential voices are expressing dissatisfaction with the current situation, and this is enough for me to push ahead. I stress that I want to work with both sides because it is obvious that this negative relationship has taken a high toll over the years. "I only need to interview a handful of people saying things like, 'It's lousy and I'm not happy but it's a job,' and 'I hate coming to work because there's so much tension,' to hear how unpleasant the work climate is," I say. I reiterate that in such situations no one wins, and each clash just adds a new layer of defensiveness and resentment. "There's got to be a better way," I suggest. In response, I receive nods of encouragement.

I get the go-ahead from the union for a very informal meeting with four representatives from each side to address whether we ought to proceed and if so, how. Although the concept of cooperative efforts is now circulating, the time is not ripe. After an introductory meeting, Carl announces that they still are not interested in continuing at this time. Apparently, the talks are still viewed as a management ploy to get the union to lower its guard.

Some months later, the union and management engage in collective bargaining. Despite a failure to get union leadership to sign on to a new cooperative process, Jen continues her efforts unilaterally. She believes the acrimonious conflict in much of the union-management relationship is keeping her from doing her job as well as she can, and she is dissatisfied in her "tough guy" role. Jen hires a new lawyer-negotiator who is comfortable with "mutual gains" bargaining styles (as opposed to adversarial bargaining). She begins to design a different approach to the negotiations, informing union leadership of her actions and intentions at each step. The results are significant, and at the conclusion of the negotiations, perhaps the best ever in the history of the organization, the process is described as having been "harmonious."

A new cooperative vocabulary has been introduced into the adversarial relations; a new opportunity has been created. Still, change is incremental at best. The process of "changing cultures" from a decades-long legacy of adversarial methods and attitudes to cooperative ones cannot happen in one great leap.

Scene Two: Conflict Within the Union

The first call for help comes from the base of the organizational pyramid. The clerical staff is at each other's throats. They are plagued by gossip, high turnover, and absenteeism, and most feel overworked and undersupported, both by their bosses and each other. Trouble comes to a head when two receptionists have a shouting match in front of patients. Jen tells Katherine, the team leader of the clerical staff, to either discipline the staff or get rid of them. Katherine, who is also the incoming union president, suggests that this might be a good time to bring in the outside consultant (me) Jen had introduced some months ago. "If you discipline these workers, I think you know there will be unpleasant ramifications from the union side," Katherine tells Jen. Jen is delighted, however, that her previous efforts to get actors in the system to take responsibility for change might finally bear fruit. "Too bad it had to come from a crisis, but I'm glad it came," she reports in a phone call to me.

In organizations, intragroup dynamics (dynamics within groups) interplay powerfully upon intergroup dynamics (dynamics between groups). Although such dynamics can and must be constructive if an organization is to be most healthy and efficient, they more often than not are destructive. The first place to look to launch a constructive conflict engagement process in a firm plagued by intransigent conflict is not between but within groups. While intergroup conflicts are regularly manifest and troubling, under the surface there often lurk latent or hidden intragroup conflicts that fuel or at least sustain the former.

After holding discussions with staff and the managers of the clerical unit in conflict, I again find clear signals of an intransigent conflict. Everyone is blaming everyone else. Morale is low. Turnover is high. Rancor and dissatisfaction are obvious, and apparently it has been ongoing for many years. To begin, we organize a one-day retreat to surface some of the workers' frustrations.

Framing Visions and Barriers. We begin the retreat with a round-robin of visions about what their work lives might be under the best of circumstances.

Instead of starting with antagonistic venting and moving into reflexive reframing, the visions-barriers process used here in an intragroup setting achieves some of the same goals without the acrimonious process. In intragroup situations, rancor is often interpersonal and can be distracting to the task of changing the context or system within which such animosity often flourishes. Unlike intergroup situations, in which an adversarial framing process can help move backward (venting) before moving forward (expressing hopes and needs), it is not as fruitful in intragroup conflicts, in part due to the delicacy and weight of interpersonal relations within groups. Thus getting participants to voice positive visions is safer for preserving ongoing relationships and helps create a context and motivation to work together better as a team and to try to make these visions a reality.

Here are some of the responses I get when I ask for visions of how the hospital workers would like to see their work life:

- "I would like to be proud of what I do here."

- "I want to be more involved in what goes on in our unit and how things function. I'd like to be asked my opinion more often."

- "I would like to see an environment in which everyone takes responsibility for success instead of passing the buck and blaming each other for failure."

A secretary named Linda demurs, saying she feels too angry to express positive visions. "This all seems beside the point. People here are messing with my life, and I won't take it any more." I urge Linda to talk a bit more about this anger and what would have to be different to overcome it. "There is so much gossiping and back-biting here that I feel like I am either directly or indirectly under attack all the time," she says. "I can't function in such a situation. I don't believe it's possible, but we need an environment in which people would be open, honest, and supportive of each other." She has worked her way around to defining a vision as the opposite of what angers her so much. Another worker agrees. "There needs to be more respect for each other; we need somehow to build more trust and open communication."

I ask them now to explore the barriers to achieving these visions. Here are some of their responses:

- Lack of recognition or appreciation for work done

- Workload stress and home stress

- Gossiping, mistrust, and rumors

- Lack of clear roles, tasks, and functions

- Lack of time to be creative

- An Us-versus-Them attitude

We then group these visions and barriers into four issues: identity, teamwork, work environment and atmosphere, and trust and communication.

Inventing. We next hold a session to invent ways to overcome the barriers to achieving their visions. After I explain the concept of integrative problem solving, the participants divide into teams to propose solutions to these four categories of broad problems. Upon completion of the proposals, each group reports back to the whole on their suggestions for working toward fulfilling their visions.

The group that worked on identity problems suggests, among other things, that employees be called "coworkers" instead of "A.M./P.M. shift employees," which is viewed as divisive. The group addressing teamwork proposes to develop clearer agreements regarding job functions, roles, and tasks so that everyone in the work unit can share expectations and norms about who is doing what, why, and how. The group established to improve the work atmosphere proposes new guidelines for how workers should confront each other directly instead of through back-biting and gossiping. And the group whose goal is to foster further trust and communication proposes that what the union team has learned during the past few months about its own functioning can provide a model for a new kind of open and honest relationship that management has been insisting it wants.

Action Planning. Finally, the union groups begin to develop ways to implement and sustain the inventions they have formulated:

Identity problems. To help the staff affirmatively answer the questions, Who are we? and What do we care about?, a coordinating council is established to promote and tend to their needs. Its first order of business is to oversee, refine, implement, and sustain some of the inventions that the staff has come up with during this retreat. It is to be constituted, on a rotating basis, of all staff members. The primary objective of this group is to maintain and further consolidate intragroup identity and solidarity, while also coordinating and cooperating with management for improving the work life and satisfaction of all. This committee will be charged with further developing and implementing some of the proposed ideas.

Teamwork. It is clear that one of the key barriers to effective teamwork in this unit is a lack of clarity and commitment to functions, roles, and tasks. This group undertakes a process to remedy that. With my guidance, the workers employ a *reflexive role renego-tiation* process to create inner commitment and shared understanding of who is to do what, when, why, and how, and with what kind of support (see Exhibit 7.1). They gather data about all the tasks expected of the unit and about who is responsible for doing what. This baseline articulation of goals, roles, and expectations sets the stage for ongoing renegotiation. Next, team members express their professional values and state why they do or do not want to do what they do. Now they begin to renegotiate who does what, by giving away or taking on new roles and responsibilities that best suit their professional competence, motivations, and values. This then builds internal stability and commitment within the team and among all members. Next, prepared for constructive conflict, they are flexible and proactive about needed changes in the agreements they have fostered about who does what, when, why, and how. They return on a regular basis to re-articulate who does what, when, why, and how. An ideally functioning team is one that plans its change proactively and engages in conflict as a vehicle for dynamism and growth.

Improve atmosphere. To foster a better work environment, the support committee adapts an instrument to proactively address interpersonal anger and misunderstandings before they fester and

Exhibit 7.1. Reflexive Role Renegotiation.

Gather data about goals, roles, and task expectations.

Articulate professional motivations and values.

Renegotiate roles and task expectations
according to values, preferences, and competency.

Prepare for constructive conflict and return to data gathering
and renegotiating on a regular basis.

Source: Adapted from Sherwood and Glidewell's "Pinchpoint" model (1983).

degenerate into the kind of shouting match that had launched this intervention in the first place. They come up with a system whereby when staff members begin to feel a conflict over any issue, large or small, with any other staffer, they will send him or her a *conflict engagement form*. This will lead to a direct or facilitated encounter, depending upon the wishes of the initiator. There will then be a dis-cussion, beginning with some statements of mutual appreciation or respect (for example, "I value the work you do for this hospital"), fol-lowed by an exploration of the issue as presented (antagonistic fram-ing, though in a nonvolatile manner). At this discussion the initiator is expected to amplify on the single concern that is raised in the notice (the discussion is intended to be focused and straightforward; if it is more complex or volatile, a different, facilitated process is used by requesting that a facilitator convene and structure discussions). The coworkers will then seek to arrive at a shared and inclusive understanding of the issue (reflexive reframing) and begin generat-ing possible solutions (inventing). Finally, they write a brief sum-mary of the process used, the new understandings achieved, and their agreements (if needed) for different behavior (action planning).

For example, the process could work as follows. A secretary's office mate was taking resource materials (pencils) from her desk without either asking for or replacing them. When the two got together, the taker acknowledged the other secretary's concerns, told her she hadn't known it bothered her so much, and would be careful in the future. (See Exhibit 7.2.) This small conflict could have escalated. Instead it served to open lines of effective communication between coworkers. Instead of turning into large issues, when small problems are proactively engaged in this way they can become opportunities for team building. "It's amazing how in a short time we were talking with each other a lot and enjoying each other's company so much more."[1]

Trust and communication. Proud of their own accomplishments and prodded by Katherine, the union proposes expanding their circle by initiating discussions with management about how to

Exhibit 7.2. Conflict Engagement Form.

To: Jane from Clara

I. *Issue:* Concern about lack of respect for my materials.

Need for facilitator: Yes___ No: __X__

Proposed time and place: Staff Room, 10:00 A.M., 9/9/99

First Choice

Staff room on Monday morning

Second Choice

Staff room breakfast Tuesday

Third Choice

You Suggest

_____

II. *Shared analysis of causes:*

Jane has been stepping on Clara's toes without knowing it. Clara feels disregarded by Jane's actions; Clara now understands that Jane meant her no harm but had different expectations about supplies.

III. *Description of process used and agreement (if any needed) reached:*

Clara expressed appreciation for Jane's work style and efficiency but said she was beginning to feel resentful about her things not being respected. She said it felt like she was not respected. Jane expressed surprise that her behavior was offensive and said she felt materials belonged to everyone, not anyone in particular. However, understanding how it made Clara feel, she was willing to try to correct her behavior in this regard and hoped they could get on with building their friendship back to where it had been. Jane said it was fine for Clara to give her gentle reminders if she started to slip. She was glad to know that there was a specific problem that had been blocking this friendship, since previously it had seemed so promising and satisfying.

decrease the legacy of rancor and malevolence that has plagued their relations for so long. No longer feeling like problem children in the organization, they instead view themselves as a model for organizational effectiveness and worker satisfaction and want to share what they know.

By the time the intervention is over, one of the participants exclaims, "A miracle has happened!" Clearly, the clerical staff was a group ready for change. Several months later when I return to see how things are going, the group is upbeat, proud, and tremendously unified. The success of this initiative does indeed reverberate around the entire organization, from the bottom up.

Act Two: Transformation Within Management

Scene One: Another Pause on the Way to Improved Intergroup Relations

Several months later Katherine approaches Jen and says it might be a good time to reconsider an educational meeting to explore deepening union-management cooperation. Jen is thrilled. However, ever the student of good lessons, she thinks that just as the union had spent time to get their own house in order, so management should also do some homework, especially given a recent confrontation between two upper-level managers.

Two upper-level managers, Fred and Richard, were arguing over their responsibilities on a project to develop a new center in conjunction with a research university. Fred claimed he was being blamed for the other's incompetence; Richard accused Fred of selling the project by hooking the potential partners with unrealistic promises, thus leaving Richard holding the bag. As the debate heated up and the two men raised their voices and moved toward one another, a shoving match broke out and ended with one of them landing on the floor. Although in fact he had simply missed his footing, soon the place was buzzing. "Richard decked him!" "They drew blood." "These are our leaders?!"

Although the two managers involved in the scuffle actually had a productive discussion after venting their anger, the rest of the management and staff was left feeling like the place was going crazy. Said one of the chief executives, "This hospital needs a hospital!"

John, the hospital director, is at his wit's end when he calls on Jen to help. Reflecting on the good work the union team had done, Jen then calls me and asks me to conduct similar workshops for the management team. In particular, she seeks help in handling Fred, who seems to be having conflicts with everyone. I am direct about my theory of practice—that when called in to address a conflict that is presumably caused by one villain, I try first to broaden the view.

Although disputants often blame others for a conflict, I try to get them to accept some measure of personal responsibility. Blame is often attached unrealistically to individuals, with self-righteous claims such as, "If only they could get their act together and grow up . . . " I repeatedly explain that one individual is rarely at fault in organizational conflict; rather the behavior is often symptomatic of wider system dysfunctions. The acting out of one individual, particularly if that individual is a key player, is frequently a sign that the whole system needs attention.

I offer to undertake a *conflict audit* of the management team to frame the problems and to explore what opportunities for change and growth are being missed. This begins with interviews with a dozen upper-level managers. Over and over again, many point to Fred as the major problem. After some probing, however, it becomes increasingly clear that Fred (and the way he is scapegoated) has become a fulcrum for precisely the pattern of stress and blame that is dragging the hospital down. One manager tells me, "I hate coming to the office. I feel instantly pulled under, on guard, suspicious, and I become mean. It's a defensive reaction; I join various coalitions since that's how one gets ahead around here."

"You mean you get ahead by putting others behind?," I ask. "Yeah. It's lousy isn't it?"

At a management committee meeting I was invited to observe one week later, a vice president named George takes the floor to say he is fed up with materials being circulated when they contain misspellings. As an example he uses the proposal for partnering with the research university. He feels that those at fault should be found and fired to serve as a lesson to others. "It is unacceptable that we produce such amateurish reports. Clearly, we have incompetent individuals on our staff, and we must get rid of them." Others agree.

I scratch my head and continue to watch as a kind of mob mentality emerges. These senior managers are wasting a tremendous amount of valuable meeting time venting their anger against incompetent employees who cannot spell, or at least do not adequately proofread their work. It is time for a formal conflict audit.

Scene Two: Executive Conflict Audit— Discovering Blame and Projection

The executive conflict audit consists of summaries of interviews based on several simple questions: What do you think are the main problems in terms of human relationships? Are there any related problems in terms of structural arrangements?

I begin the audit by asking these questions of upper-level managers. Within a few days a number of managers say that things are already changing for the better and ask me how I had managed it. In fact I had done nothing more than ask these simple questions and listen empathically. This alone provides a catharsis for some managers who are able to get some weight off their chest. In addition, simply concentrating on these ongoing problems gives the firm a sense of volition about them. "Everyone seems to be a bit more self-conscious and considerate all of a sudden," says one manager. No longer is the environment simply nefarious; rather they can now begin to identify the problems. At this point it does not matter that many are still calling for Fred to leave, or for employees who cannot spell to be fired, and so forth. A more accurate definition of the issues will come later. Nearly all the managers are extreme Type A personalities who seem to strive for an unrealistic perfectionism, resulting in a sense that mistakes are unacceptable and have to be either covered up or blamed on someone else. No wonder the staff constantly feels on-guard and under attack.

Audit Summary. At a meeting with management I report my findings from the audit, summarized in Exhibit 7.3, distinguishing the social-emotional issues from the task and structural issues. After reviewing this summary, the managers are surprised at how much is on the left side of the list and how little is on the right side. Still, they confirm that it is an accurate representation of the state of the firm.

Now it is the managers' turn to express their visions of new behavior that would make the office a better work environment. Many of the responses illuminate the same issues that the clerical staff highlighted:

- "More sensitivity to each other's nerve endings is needed."

- "Stop always looking over each other's shoulders."

- "We need to show respect and trust that everyone will do the right thing to the best of their ability."

- "Eliminate the rumor mill."

- "I wish I didn't have to mediate conflicts between other people—that they could talk to each other openly and directly."

- "It would be nice if everyone here felt they were treated fairly and equitably."

Exhibit 7.3. The Conflict Audit.

Social-Emotional Issues	Task-Structural Issues
(including interpersonal relations, group dynamics, culture, atmosphere, communication, morale)	(including roles, tasks, functions, authority, responsibility)
Grudges	*Fuzzy job descriptions*
• Carrying burden of history and perceptions of past slights	• Unclear roles, tasks, functions
Erratic or poor communication	*Unclear lines of authority*
• Don't argue constructively	• Don't know where the buck stops
• Poor giving and receiving criticism	*Unarticulated rules and codes of conduct*
Mistrust	• Everyone behaves according to themselves
• Fairness issues	*Poor decision-making processes and means of implementation*
• Coalitions	• They take forever and often lead to unsatisfactory outcomes
Back-biting culture	
• Blaming	
• Undermining	
• Gossip	
Volatility	
• "A time bomb"	
• "Constant border wars"	
Lack of common vision	
• Don't agree on who we are, what our values are, and what we care about	

- "I need more time to do creative work."

- "More delegation of authority and responsibility from top to midlevel management would help."

With the identification of problems, some hope for change begins to grow. This is both promising and risky. My job now is to help move them from blame to acceptance of responsibility.

Scene Three: Reflexive Reframing—Change from the Inside Out

To model a change process starting from the inside out, the three senior managers arrange several meetings with me to address old wounds and think about new relationships. The goal is for each manager of this executive committee to take responsibility instead of leveling blame.

During one of these meetings one of the chief executives, Mike, says it has become clear that the way top management handles relations—with mistrust, poor communication, little candor, and a lot of back-biting and coalition building—has generalized throughout the organization. "We are committing ourselves to change and we will ask, in large measure by modeling, for change in the way we all relate to each other." he says.

John concurs, and he reiterates that the hospital is at a potential turning point. "The changes around here have to start with each of us. The idea of us modeling a new level of respectful communication throughout the hospital by doing it among ourselves is right on target. Changes around here will not occur if each of us points to the other and says, 'He's the problem.' I'd like to get all of you on board to help," he urges. Later the top managers present the outcomes of these sessions to the management committee, describing how they are amazed by some of the misperceptions their colleagues have held about the meaning of past events and how these misunderstandings have persisted for years. They say they feel like they have cleared the air and are truly ready to start acting and leading like a team.

Exhibit 7.4. John's Overhead Chart.

MEETING AGENDA

- Overhaul zero-sum atmosphere
- Cultivate new spirit of teamwork
- Develop new paradeim [sic]

Scene Four: The Management Retreat—A New Paradeim [*sic*]

Several months after the conflict audit, I facilitate a three-day management retreat. John opens by presenting his agenda, complete with fancy overhead illustrations (Exhibit 7.4). He says he wants to work on addressing the zero-sum atmosphere that has taken hold at Mercy Medical; he wants to cultivate a new spirit of teamwork and foster a new "paradeim" [sic] to drive and sustain these changes.

As he discusses that last item, several people around the room snicker. I jump up and say, "Now it's time to get to work meeting these goals."

I begin by pointing out that it is obvious many managers and employees take pleasure in pouncing on others who make mistakes. I tell the group they are missing a great potential resource of vitality and growth through this behavior and suggest that mistakes, like conflicts, can be resources for learning, changes, and enhancing a spirit of cooperation and teamwork. I go so far as to say that mistakes might just be the avenue by which John's admirable goals could be accomplished.

Here, a manager named Harry interrupts with a remark that provides a good way to illustrate the point I want to make. "Excuse me, Mr. Consultant, I would like to give you some friendly advice, and I'll do it for free. We are all managers here—good luck managing us!"

I point out that I am being paid for my advice and will leave when the retreat is over. I suggest he can undermine me if he wants to, but I will still get my paycheck, and he will still return to work on Monday unhappy to be there. "Maybe you want to help me instead?" I use Harry's comments to illustrate that in the firm's present culture, undercutting one another seems to pay a premium. "In reality," I say, "it takes a toll. If you would like to, you can undercut John and his agenda right now by focusing on what is wrong with it; on the other hand, you can use the same trigger as a vehicle for fulfilling the agenda itself." I then ask how John's mistake might be pointed out in a way that improves the positive, cooperative spirit that the agenda itself was designed to foster.

When one person suggests doing it in a way that does not make John defensive, a man named Stanley offers this: "John, you must have been up really late preparing for this meeting. You must have been so pressured and tired that you didn't use your spell check and look what happened—you misspelled *paradigm!*"

I ask how we can go even further and create an opportunity for learning and change from this example.

At this point one of the managers says, "When we were beating on our staff last week about misspellings in the manuals, perhaps we missed an important dynamic around this firm. We are all too stressed and don't have enough support and backup staff."

In this environment John can be open about his embarrassment over the spelling mistake without being defensive. He agrees the hospital has not figured out a way to complete projects with enough spare time left to check and double-check the work. This leads to a discussion of whether systems can be put in place to enable other employees to help out.

I am pleased to point out that the group has moved from undermining and blame to accepting responsibility for problem solving, improvements, and change. "Your culture of blame inhibits positive communication about mistakes," I continue. "This culture looks for opportunities to take shots at others. Mistakes viewed as wholly bad perpetuate the zero-sum power game: I win only as a result of your loss." I enumerate the important issues that have surfaced during this brief exchange: saving face instead of beating each other up, sharing responsibility instead of casting aspersion, and working with mistakes and conflicts as an opportunity for learning and change.

A woman named Beth goes one step further and suggests that each member of the group should examine why they get satisfaction from the mistakes of others. She wants to know why they are so quick to blame and find fault instead of working together and addressing mistakes as shared concerns. "Can people around here ask for support and admit mistakes safely?" The answer is obvious to everyone present.

Scene Five: Inventing—What Is to Be Done?

As we move into the inventing stage, the entire management team sets up temporary task forces to work on solutions to the specific obstacles the managers have articulated: gossip, lack of team spirit, lack of clarity about what is expected, and so forth. The barriers to fulfilling the hospital's objectives are divided into four groups, and task force members set about inventing ways to overcome them. These groups and their proposed solutions are as follows:

Bridging gaps and improving team spirit. To reinvent the culture of the hospital and create an environment of reduced back-biting and malicious gossip, this task force creates a Statement of Intention. "We will seek to undermine each other less, stop venting our anger indirectly, and learn to address our grievances directly to the people we are having trouble with."

Organizational definition and task delegation. Here the task force recommends establishing clear agreements about areas of responsibility and firm lines of authority of managerial tasks, roles, and functions. The hope is that, built upon such clarity, there will be more real delegation from top management to other levels.

Professional growth. This group proposes the systematic creation of opportunities to develop the intellectual capital of all employees, regardless of position. They suggest providing incentives for staff members to participate in conferences, outside courses, and development projects at other medical centers. The group calls on senior staff to model, manage, and mentor this process.

Giving 100 percent. This task force calls for creating an environment that reflects trust, respect, and accountability, leading to renewed staff energy for personal and organizational excellence. They request a clear definition of what the hospital means by "100 percent." Are they referring to effort or outcome? How can it be measured, and how can a shared value of excellence be fostered?

Scene Six: Action Planning: Who Is to Do What, When, and How?

Each task force comes up with plans to enact their proposed solutions, and over the next several months there is a great deal of activity and excitement at Mercy Medical. They sustain change in two areas—bridging gaps and organizational definition and delegation. The other areas are set aside for the time being because of daily work pressures involved in getting routine work done. *This is also a reflection of the limited threshold of many organizations for implementing change at a number of levels simultaneously.* The hope is that as the first two areas of change take hold, the others will move to center stage.

Bridging Gaps: Jay's Rule. To provide a concrete example of taking action, I have a suggestion for the task force concentrating on bridging gaps. I propose that they ask management to accept and model a new norm for interpersonal communication on a trial basis; it consists of a commitment by management to strive to communicate calmly and directly to any employee or group with whom a conflict has arisen. Although I intend this suggestion only as a possible example to get the ball rolling, the task force reacts with great enthusiasm. It recommends that management commit itself immediately, on a month-long trial basis, to stop (1) accepting or participating in back-biting, (2) indirect venting, (3) undermining one another, and (4) rumor mongering. This challenge takes on a life of its own, and soon the hospital is buzzing about Jay's Rule.

Some employees are excited and view the effort as a step in the right direction. "It's about time we enforce some new norms for human decency around here," one says. Others are uncomfortable with it and view it as debilitating self-censorship. "If we can't speak with candor about our problems and get support from others not in the conflict with us, we will simply suppress them until we blow up," another says.

Management does indeed report a greater level of self-consciousness for the month-long trial period. One senior executive tells me, "At least I know when I am breaking Jay's Rule." When they introduce the concept to the entire hospital staff, they decide to rename it a "Communication Goal" rather than a hard-and-fast rule that has to be followed. Management is quite cognizant that sometimes indirect venting is a necessary safety valve, particularly if a member of the staff feels unable to speak directly to a manager about a conflict. They further realize that the main goal is not really to promote strict adherence to four thou-shalt-nots but to create a space free of the unproductive culture of back-biting and gossip by generating a heightened self-awareness of the negative norm. The aim is to foster alternative ways of talking about interpersonal problems so that new, creative relationships and problem solving can evolve.

Definition and Delegation: Role Clarification. Having addressed a number of social and emotional issues in the first months of this intervention, we begin to set up a process of planned renegotiation around managers' roles, tasks, and functions. It was clear from the beginning that part of the suspicion and discomfort in the hospital derived not only from poor communication patterns but also from a lack of clarity about who was doing what, when, how, and why. I use the same reflexive role renegotiation process I had employed with the clerical workers to good effect. After using the process for a while, again with Jen's initiative, the management team formally adopts it as its own and uses it regularly.

Act Three: Transformation Between Union and Management

Jen calls Katherine to tell her, "We're ready." Specifically, Jen inquires about whether the *notice of conflict* model that has been used within the clerical staff so effectively could become a useful vehicle for transforming relations between management and the union. Katherine is a bit skeptical. "Don't you think we had better start from the beginning and evolve our own ways as we go?" Jen agrees.

Scene One: The Prenegotiation Meeting

The stated goal of this process, bringing together union leaders and key managers, is "learning to communicate better with each other while building more trust in each other and dealing more honestly with each other."

In the short run the participants' stated goals are to further improve communication both within teams and between union and management, learn to stop personalizing spontaneous conflicts, gain skills and perspective to stop turning conflicts into crises, and articulate differences and determine areas of agreement.

Antagonism. I begin by asking the participants to map out some of the problems in the union-management relationship, telling them I want them to be able to get some of their grievances off their chests. "If we don't clear the air a bit, there may not be much room available for establishing new modes of interaction in the future," I say. "So if something about the relationship bogs you down, tell us. If you feel wounded by something, please share it as specifically as possible."

One union member jumps in and raises what he sees as a key problem—mistrust and rumors. "I don't feel very easy about opening myself up and stating my grievances, both because I'm not sure it won't be used against me by people in this meeting, or that it won't get out to folks outside."

In setting up the ground rules of the meeting, I had stressed that this session was private and off the record so participants could feel free to explore new ideas and unfreeze old patterns. However, this comment gives me both the push and the green light to focus on this issue further. I say I am glad he has raised the issue and I explain the need for strict confidentiality. "In my meetings participants regularly say this isn't necessary and that anything they say in this room they would be happy for people outside to hear," I continue. "But I insist that all present accept the ground rules of confidentiality and nonattribution, because this is an exploratory meeting and it needs to be fully free-spirited and nonbinding." I explain that participants would, perhaps unconsciously, restrict their flexibility and creativity if they felt like their respective constituencies were metaphorically peering over their shoulders. I indicate that at the end of the day we will decide how we will communicate with others about the content and outcomes of the meeting. "Clearly, when you talk about the need for rumor control, it behooves us to share as much information in as careful a way as is possible to help others come along with you on this journey," I say. "For us to do good work though, I really must insist to start with on the confidentiality and nonattribution rules."

After getting everyone's agreement, I direct the process back to antagonistic framing. Here is a summary of the gripes that come out:

- Small conflicts turn into major crises.

- Rumors escalate, and premature conclusions are made about facts or events.

- Things seem to be muddled, sometimes on purpose, and lies are told.

- There is a sense that someone up top doesn't care. When one of us is treated badly, each of us feels like we're next. I can't tell you what this does to morale.

- There is a lack of appreciation for work well done around here. Sadly, though, I'm used to it.

- When the next major conflict erupts, are we going to get along?

- Problem-solving mechanisms and available avenues are often under-utilized.

- Decisions are made by fiat.

- We are blamed for past events and the troubled legacy between union and management that we had nothing to do with.

- Intragroup conflicts—envy, taking sides, personality clashes—lead to poor intergroup relations.

Resonance. Now it is time to examine the underlying causes of the dynamics at work in this conflict. First we hold a dialogue during which union and management leaders are quite open about their hopes and fears in their work relationship. Next we develop a list of presenting problems and causes, summarizing the needs that are threatened or frustrated in their relationship. Exhibit 7.5 shows the results.

Exhibit 7.5. The Conflict's Underlying Causes.

Conflict Manifestation	Underlying Causes
Every conflict is a crisis	Lack of proactive conflict engagement (conflict dynamics negative)
Rumors and back-biting are common	Sense of powerlessness and lack of control; getting ahead through joining coalitions against other coalitions
Muddles and lies circulate	Truth-telling not rewarded (deceit seems to be)
Mistakes are seen as grave offenses	Punitive culture
Competition reigns	Low team spirit; poor modeling (executive management competes)
Decisions are made by fiat	Lack of participation

Given the analytic clarity that participants demonstrate in articulating both the symptoms and underlying causes of their conflict, it seems reasonable to expect them to start renegotiating their relationships so they can address their problems cooperatively.

Inventing. Now it is time to invent some solutions. I begin by asking each side to generate possible solutions for overcoming the conflict manifestations, stressing that their solutions should also address the underlying causes they have articulated. "Brainstorm solutions you believe will effectively address some of the symptoms and the causes," I say. "Your task at this point is just to outline the broad parameters of solutions, keeping your own constituency in mind as you go." I indicate that later in this phase they will share their outlined solutions with the other side, and they will then form joint working teams to structure detailed solution development and implementation plans.

The union side first tackles the problem of muddles and lies. Their proposed solutions are:

- Provide vehicles for thorough and easy access to information in the early stages of a rumor mill; for example, hold regular organizational meetings for all management and staff.

- Develop an information hotline, and put suggestion boxes in accessible places.

- Keep everyone informed of substantive changes in the system. Ideally this should occur in the planning stages but is critical when changes are implemented.

To address the problem of lack of appreciation, the union side has several suggestions:

- Hold a system-wide Appreciation Day once a year.

- Educate various sectors of the organization about each other.

- Plan joint after-work activities such as retreats, sporting events, or discussion groups.

To reduce the adversarial culture of Us versus Them, the union participants recommend holding regular meetings facilitated by an outside consultant. They see this as a way to continue the search for new ways to solve old problems.

The management group focuses on two of the same major areas of the conflict: lack of appreciation and the culture of adversarial relations. Their inventions for creating a greater sense of recognition are:

- Provide mechanisms for regularized employee recognition.

- Engage in job swaps within labor groups and between labor and management groups.

- Sponsor a system-wide meeting at the beginning of every year in which joint union-management teams will give presentations about our shared enterprise, goals, norms, and accomplishments.

The management group believes that the antagonistic nature of relations at the hospital both represents and causes many other problems. To help combat this, they come up with these recommendations:

- Hold monthly union-management meetings. The agendas must be pre-set by all participants, and all must agree to abide by jointly determined rules of order and conduct.

- Initiate joint projects, both social and educational.

- Establish a joint task force to evaluate problems as they arise and before they become crises.

- Set up team sports activities with a mix of union and management players on each team.

- Arrange for a lunch-time joke exchange program.

Action Planning. As we move into setting a plan for action, I set up four mixed groups of union and management members to design more detailed plans for refining and implementing their inventions. Two groups address the problem of lack of appreciation, and the other two groups focus on the adversarial relationships between union and management. I ask them to consider the following variables and provide in summary form a programmatic description for the whole group to consider and refine: What should be done?, Why?, When?, Who should do it?, and How? The goal is to design solutions so that members of each side will see them as appealing and useful and will therefore be supportive and enthusiastic. Most important in this cooperative problem-solving effort, each side needs to take care to address the underlying causes of the conflict as well as the specific conflict manifestations at hand.

One of the first plans proposed is to create a parallel structure in the form of a union-management council, symbolically calling it "HUMANCIL." This title demonstrates both that the council is constituted of the distinct groups—union and management (u-man), which seek to retain their separate identities, but also that they are linked by an overarching (human)ity. This council would meet regularly like a support group, with the purpose of enhancing relations and initiating cooperative problem-solving efforts. This idea is outlined in Exhibit 7.6.

After agreeing to establish this parallel structure, the group further articulates its functions by expanding to other problem areas they had defined earlier, such as the example in Exhibit 7.7.

Scene Two: Driving Progress Throughout the Hospital Stalled

HUMANCIL meets on a monthly basis and begins to build greater trust between union and management members. They plan educa-

Exhibit 7.6. Proposed Solution for Adversarial Relations.

Problem: Adversarial Mode of Relationships and Problem Solving

What: Hold monthly meetings of a cooperative body under the new, shared name of HUMANCIL—the union-management council.

Why: To promote communication and the sharing of information in order to solve problems proactively and cooperatively; to build trust, empower participants, promote hope, and provide a model for problem solving for the rest of the system.

Who: Executive board of union and management team.

How: The first meeting will work on establishing ground rules and procedures for future meetings. This may include ways to set agendas through input from various constituencies. During this phase, begin to prioritize recommendations for further development and implementation of proposed ideas.

---

tional meetings for both union and management constituencies, hoping to build a sense of inclusion. In addition, plans are made for a HUMANCIL newsletter, suggestion boxes, community-wide forums, and celebration and appreciation days to be sponsored by HUMANCIL. However, only a few of these plans are carried out. Although HUMANCIL forges a new feeling of teamwork between union and management leaders, such organizational learning and progress is not adequately generalized throughout the hospital. While a satisfying experience for its members, HUMANCIL never gains sufficient legitimacy for its new ways of doing things. This is a significant dilemma that stalls progress at lower levels of the hospital, even as change occurs at the top. Within the rank and file, a rebellion begins to brew.

When I next return several months later, I find serious problems. The parallel structure of HUMANCIL has been functioning effectively—almost too effectively. It has begun to replace the formal conflict management procedure—the grievance process—without gaining the external sanction to do so. Moreover, though the new

Exhibit 7.7. Proposed Solution for Lack of Appreciation.

Problem: Lack of Appreciation Within and Between Labor and Management Groups

What: Foster mutual appreciation.

Why: Because each unit rarely knows about the good efforts of the other, and even more rarely expresses appreciation for the other. This is part of the reason for low morale, which needs boosting from within. It is necessary to enhance mutual appreciation and increase morale throughout the system.

Who: Various segments of union and management groups, especially those with the lowest morale. These groups will be identified by HUMANCIL.

How: Various labor and management teams, to be identified by HUMANCIL, will be honored publicly for their efforts. We will establish a monthly social hour, and at that occasion the good work of a selected group will be spotlighted. All members of the unit will be invited to step up and receive recognition.

---

inner circle (a newly formed intragroup dynamic) has learned to cooperate successfully, the outer group (notably the union members) feel they are being abandoned by their leaders. Because I am an outside consultant and visit only every few months, I can provide only irregular vigilance and guidance. HUMANCIL was designed to serve as an overseer and catalyst, but it lost its way as it began to become an alternative, somewhat dissociated, structure. Instead of focusing on the specific steps and strategies we had designed, HUMANCIL has become, somewhat unwittingly, something of a formal conflict prevention body. In a way the good work of HUMANCIL proves to be its own undoing.

During a two-day workshop held to lay the groundwork for upcoming contract negotiations, the union leadership reports a serious lack of support from its membership. Although HUMANCIL has managed to head off a number of union grievances, usually when they were relatively small and could be ameliorated by proactive communication and problem solving, the perception is that the union is losing grievances more often than before. Often these simple grievances would previously have been "won" by the union. Now the total number of grievances heard has been reduced, and the simple ones that the union previously could count as successes are no longer making it to the formal grievance process. It has begun to appear that the union is losing more often than winning. Some workers are beginning to feel that their leaders are becoming too cozy with management. "I have been called a traitor and accused of sleeping with the enemy," reports one union leader, who feels vulnerable to the charge that cooperation with management could harm the union's interests in the contract negotiations. The union leadership is unable to persuade the rank and file to join with them in viewing management as allies instead of adversaries. The leaders feel that without the consent of their members, they have no legitimacy to pursue this path. Their efforts are halted. HUMANCIL is dismantled and my intervention ends on an exhale.

Epilogue

A number of important benefits and lessons came out of this lengthy journey (nearly three years in all) at Mercy Medical. First of all, as the union and management headed into a new round of negotiations several months later, the cooperative momentum between them was very evident, and both the process and outcomes of the negotiation were viewed as cooperative and mutually beneficial. More important, a prevailing sense of overarching team spirit within the union and management groups remained. However, although union rank and file appreciated their contract, and their suspicions about their own leadership were greatly reduced, antagonism between them and management was still fairly high. Perhaps solace may be found in the fact that, as Yeats wrote, "Peace comes dropping slowly." It does appear, now several years after this intervention, that union-management relations throughout the hospital are thawing.

Unifying Themes in Identity Conflict in Organizations

Drawing out a number of common threads within and between groups in organizational conflict can serve to conclude this chapter. First of all, the chapter illustrates how a meshing of narratives *between* groups locked in identity conflict must often begin with new resonance *within* each group in the conflict.

Entry and Inclusion: Within

One common theme is the process of entry and engagement. A key lesson of this intervention end-game is that it is crucial for members of a group to gain new solidarity, not in opposition to an "other" but within themselves, if they are to become engaged in the process of dealing interactively with their conflict and with the other side. This is also one of the most difficult aspects of the conflict transformation process. Some participants will find reasons for not entering into the process, claiming that the other side is the problem and work "at home" is not the point. At the end of this intervention when the new relationship achieved between union and management was ready to be filtered down, particularly to the union rank and file, one of the organizers of the rebellion against the union leadership and the change process was a "wanna-be leader" who had not been elected several times previously. Such politics often prevails in the delicate process of culture change from confrontation to cooperation. The dissatisfied and disenfranchised may often resist change coming in from the outside, especially if they have not engaged in any change themselves. However, for internal resistance to succeed, discontent must be fairly widespread. At Mercy Medical the rank-and-file workers remained deeply suspicious and ultimately refused to allow their leaders to proceed any further in the process. Beginning a journey of reconciliation can be unsettling; people will often stay with the enemy they know rather than risk a future they do not.

As a consultant I am now much more vigilant about being inclusive in all my organizational interventions. I recently conducted an intervention at a sales firm that had grown faster than expected and was facing a crisis of leadership and confidence. After undertaking an executive conflict audit and before planning any kind of ARIA intervention at the upper level, I conducted a firm-wide worker conflict audit, which contributed directly to the leadership intervention design. At regular intervals during my meetings with top managers, we met with key workers to report on our activities and progress and to listen to their questions, comments, and concerns. It was very effective in fostering a sense of inclusiveness and building firm-wide commitment to the changes management was seeking.

It can be useful to demonstrate in small ways how powerful the process can be, then move full steam ahead. But sometimes disputants must be cajoled and persuaded to join in. It helps to remind and demonstrate to everyone that there is much to be gained on all sides.

Creativity: Within

When conflicts have protracted between groups, new life can be pumped into such relationships if dynamism and creativity can be restored within them first. Although conflict has much potential for destructiveness, it has an equal and opposite propensity to promote creativity and dynamism. As in physics, there is a need for just the right amount of friction to stimulate creativity. No work in conflict engagement is straightforward or easy, but each successful experience with it is another step toward a new legacy of transforming conflict into opportunity.

Learning: Between

A central pillar of conflict management is that it is a vehicle for constant growth and learning. Just as an individual has a memory and the capacity to learn, so too can groups in organizations and institutions learn. While conflicts within groups often have internal roots, the external sources of conflict between groups can often provide a stimulus for learning. Just as the good battle is often engaging, so too the process and promise of learning often helps opponents stick with a conflict engagement process even when it is uncomfortable. In each of the interventions examined in this chapter, a common driver for continued engagement was the memory of how unpleasant the work environment had been. I frequently hear participants at conflict resolution sessions say, "Things can't get any worse." They know that their traditional patterns of behavior are not useful and therefore gain the commitment to learn a better way.

Humanizing: Between

Teamwork and cooperation are often outgrowths of a process of humanizing the other side. Conflict feeds on stereotyping, projections, and negative attributions. Dehumanization is what makes intransigent conflict possible. Conflict transformation depends upon the ability of disputants to see beyond their differences, though it is not necessary to disregard differences. But when adversaries are able to step up to the balcony and observe their differences, they often discover a common, universal, and human dimension of relationships. It is, after all, this shared humanity that has made the conflict so powerful and important in the first place.

Commitment: Within and Between

A new sense of purpose and renewed commitment can grow out of the dissonance of conflict. All too often in organizations, conflict avoidance is the norm as employees react to the stress by closing down and turning away from one another. Such reactions can only lead to burn-out and dissociation. Conflict engagement can help to stimulate new commitment within groups that can lead to changed dynamics between various organizational actors and increased enthusiasm for the organizational goals of sustaining good relationships and productivity. It can help to generate a new sense of commitment; however, there must be some initial thrust and compelling commitment to change, and that is not always easy to come by.

In the labor-management conflict at Mercy, we saw this through the efforts of Jen, the vice president, who asserted that either the situation would have to improve or she would leave. She engendered a positive sense that all sides were working together for mutual gains such that the work environment would be better for everyone. In the example of the sales firm the partners handled this issue of commitment and purpose quite well, largely because they were a conflict-positive organization to begin with and did not wait until things got out of hand to address their problems. By being forthright with employees and stressing that their opinions were important, the firm's founder built a true and powerful sense of teamwork.

Teamwork: Within and Between

The importance of teamwork and collaboration is a crucial element in all areas of conflict engagement. This is why so much of the ARIA framework depends on digging below the surface of an adversarial relationship to find shared goals and values. When groups in conflict can begin by doing this within their own side, the possibility of continuing it with another side greatly increases. Whereas dissonance and polarization characterize the main "input" of conflict, if the conflict is well managed, a possible "output" can be the discovery of common values, purposes, needs, and motivations. These are the identity issues that fuel deep conflict. When those needs and values are uncovered, adversaries frequently discover that they share basic human concerns, which can foster a new commitment to teamwork and cooperation.

8

ARIA Tools

Lessons Drawn from Community Conflicts

This chapter serves to further illustrate the ARIA method in action while also providing pointers to practitioners. My experience has shown that, in writing, the ideas behind ARIA can sound more complex than they are in use. In this chapter I will illustrate that by giving examples of how ARIA has been, or might be, applied in a number of different community conflicts. Again, the ARIA process is not as linear as it might seem. Issues arising during one phase often cycle back to earlier phases. Because the framework weaves many different components together in a conflict resolution process, it is appropriate to pick and choose from the framework and to adapt it for specific purposes or settings. This chapter also provides several tools that may help along the way: a conflict assessment instrument, guidelines for conducting a conflict audit, and a step-by-step guide for applying the ARIA framework.

Identifying Identity Conflicts

Simply by asking disputants whether identity issues are at stake will help many realize that, in fact, they are. When addressed early and sensitively, identity issues can be the engine for constructive community participation and engagement, and for proactive problem solving. The extent to which identity issues are involved, as well as their centrality and salience (and the degree to which they have been ignored, threatened, or frustrated), must be rigorously investigated.

In communities, just as in organizations, conflicts are frequently avoided until they reach crisis proportions. When they are finally confronted, the results are often bloody—either metaphorically or in reality. Initiating relatively simple and straightforward conflict analysis can promote constructive conflict engagement and counteract such reactive avoidance or confrontation.

Community conflict, like ethnic conflict, is about identity: where you live, who your neighbors are, and how you relate to them. Although community conflict is about essential identity issues, it is frequently exacerbated by (or manifested in) poor procedures for inclusive and informed decision making. Examples of such community conflicts might be disagreement over where a home for mentally retarded adults is to be located, where a nuclear waste facility is to be built, or whether low-income housing should be developed in an established neighborhood. If an initially straightforward and tangible conflict is negotiated in a timely and effective manner, with proper sensitivity given to the human dimension of decision making, a largely functional and interest-based negotiation approach may be all that is required. However, if an initially interest-based conflict becomes protracted due to poor timing or to the use of inappropriate conflict management procedures, latent identity concerns may become more salient and in need of amelioration, or at least expression, prior to the successful application of functional conflict resolution.

Conflict Assessment

An identity conflict assessment can be a useful tool in helping analysts, third parties, or disputants themselves determine whether they are dealing primarily with an identity conflict or one that is mainly interest-based. The assessment instrument that I have developed to accompany the ARIA framework has three overlapping parts: the first determines the relative degree of intransigence; the second surfaces the underlying motivations of participants in the conflict; and the third generates a comparative analysis of the salience of identity and interest issues. This is a relative assessment. The question is not whether identity issues are at stake, because in most conflicts they are either manifest or latent to some extent. The question is really about saliency. Are the identity issues in this conflict manifest to the extent that addressing these underlying issues from the outset would be useful or necessary?

To illustrate this tool and the others that follow, I provide examples of community conflicts to which I have applied the ARIA framework in whole or in part.

A superintendent is fed up. His board is divided; six support him and his policies most of the time; four almost always vociferously oppose. He has announced that he plans to resign two years prior to his contract expiration. The board is united in its alarm over that. "Our disagreement is just politics as usual. Our fights here simply represent the different views in our community. You shouldn't take it so personally," says one of the board members on the opposing side. "Easy for you to say," responds a flushed superintendent. "I'm not sure that our community can handle another superintendent search and public battle over our school leadership so prematurely," says another board member. Glaring at the first board member who spoke previously, she concludes, "Isn't this what you've been waiting for—divide and conquer?" As for the superintendent, he says sadly, "I'm tired of all of this." Everyone stops and thinks.

Intransigence

Conflicts protract for a number of reasons. Often the cause is inadequate analysis, which leads to the application of inappropriate conflict management methods. A simple inquiry into the degree of conflict intransigence—determining how long the conflict has persisted or how often it has recurred—is a useful point of departure in beginning an assessment.

Inquiry: Over the last three to five years, how many times has this or a similar conflict dynamic resurfaced?

Response: "Every year for the last four years, two with this superintendent and the last two years with our old superintendent, we have had divided boards that have fought each other and poorly led the district. We have a legacy of hiring superintendents with stellar records who come here and fail. Something has to change."

Conflict Motivations

Exploring conflict motivations is particularly useful in stimulating constructive and reflexive conflict engagement. It can help parties begin to turn inward and look at their own concerns, moving away from unhelpful and reductionistic blaming. By asking questions about identity issues and whether they are salient, parties are likely to raise them, even if previously they had not framed their conflict in this way. But that is the point. Asking such questions can raise awareness and provide new focus.

Inquiry: If you were to describe key issues motivating this conflict, which cluster would fit most fully: competition over tangible and material interests, or threats to or frustration over human dignity, safety, control, and identity issues?

Response: "Both; we compete over whose policies for school taxation, resources, and so forth will prevail. We also continue to take each other apart and challenge the integrity and professionalism of each other."

Characteristics

Observers or disputants may also assess the key issues in a conflict situation to determine whether they fall closer on the continuum toward identity-based or interest-based issues.

It is useful to have various conflict stakeholders comparatively rate the focus, basis, and tangibility of the conflict (Figure 8.1). This can lead to an exploration of the best way to approach the conflict *as it is framed*—as an identity conflict for which reflexive dialogue and integrative inventing are useful, or as an interest-based dispute in which principled bargaining and negotiation may be most effective.

The conflict characteristics instrument is designed to launch a discussion about the underlying identity issues in a conflict between disputants, while a third party or analyst helps ascertain their saliency. This interaction between what is being researched and raising consciousness about what is at stake in a conflict is a further type of reflexivity. The action researcher (or analyst or third party)

Figure 8.1. Conflict Characteristics.

Focused on:

historical and psychocultural factors							finite goods or services		
1	2	(3)	4	5	6	7	8	9	10

Based in:

values and belief systems of disputant							socioeconomic factors like resources		
1	2	3	4	(5)	6	7	8	9	10

Goals:

intangible, complex, abstract							tangible, defined, concrete		
1	2	3	(4)	5	6	7	8	9	10

(Hypothetical average: 4.0)

and the party being researched mutually influence and are influenced by their interaction. Usually research is viewed as an objective, detached process whereby "contamination" of the subjects by the researcher is minimized as much as possible. By contrast, in action research of this sort the researcher or analyst seeks to influence the analysis of his or her reciprocators. (Note that the term *subjects* is not used. See Steir, 1991.) It is important to take seriously the possibility that identity concerns are important to the situation, even if not previously articulated as such. The "action scientist" in this approach to research seeks to contribute to knowledge generation not for its own sake but for its "emancipatory potential" (Argyris, Putnam, and Smith, 1985).

The Conflict Audit

A conflict audit is designed to give the third-party analyst necessary information about the range of conflict issues and negative affect surrounding the specific triggering issue, as well as the larger context within which it is embedded. The audit is also designed to motivate disputants to engage in a constructive conflict resolution process.

A group of church leaders, lay and professional, are in a face-off that is reverberating at all levels of their church community, making for tension and discomfort that is keeping pews empty during Sunday services. The ministers and other professionals at the large church feel a religious duty to open their church doors and kitchen to homeless people in the evenings. The lay leaders, reflecting a wide sentiment in the community, are fearful that the problem of indigence in the area will only be increased when word gets out on the street that a good bed and a hot meal are available at Holy Redeemer. "It's our calling and religious duty to help our less fortunate neighbors," states the minister. "We understand and appreciate what you're saying, but our first duty is to our children and their safety, and we fear this will compromise it," responds a lay leader.

Articulating Antagonism

The conflict audit begins with a series of interviews with people who are close to a triggering conflict. For the analyst, mediator, or community organizer or volunteer, the point of entry will usually be a situation that has reached crisis or near-crisis proportions. Either in an interactive session with key conflict stakeholders (which is preferable when possible) or in one-on-one discussions with these actors, the third party begins conflict engagement by encouraging disputants to put issues on the table.

In the church case the lay and professional leadership gather for several hours of exploratory discussion. After they blame each other and vent a bit, it becomes clear that this conflict is masking a whole series of value and priority conflicts that need to be surfaced if this once-vibrant church community is to regain its dynamism and inclusiveness.

Following the ARIA framework, opening the conflict engagement process by articulating antagonism helps surface issues and make hearts beat faster. "You may be our spiritual and professional leaders, but we are losing confidence in whether you are taking to heart our best interests," says one member of the congregation. Gripping his chair, the minister responds, "My spiritual duty is to lead where I believe God would have us go. If I can't do that, I do not belong here."

Clearly, opening up such heated issues and surfacing the deeply felt emotions around them requires a great deal of skill and caution. An antagonistic framing process should not be launched if the facilitator does not have a great deal of confidence that he or she can control the process beyond the initial venting by the disputants. There is an art to this process. I recall many times looking at a co-facilitator in such a process and whispering, "Is that enough?" We wanted disputants to surface enough of the problems adversarially so that they had been articulated, and at the same time to feel the futility of this approach. When that happens we can suggest a different mode of analysis and discussion. If we wait too long and get the blood boiling too hot, we might lose participants or have to spend a lot of time soothing hurt feelings before moving ahead. Like the physician, a mediator should have the Hippocratic oath foremost in his or her mind at this point, which is, "Above all else, do no harm."[1] However, if everyone dances around each other and their own tough reflections, these feelings will invariably surface later in ways that are inappropriate to the effort. If this happens, third parties may lose the control and authority they have at the start of the intervention when they have the full attention of participants.

Determining Motivation for Change

Many conflicts have both driving forces and restraining forces regarding conflict engagement and resolution processes. After disputants get things off their chests, particularly when this is done interactively and with skillful guidance, it is common for some to feel some catharsis. "I've been carrying this stuff around for so long, it is a great relief to be able to say it. Moreover, I am actually glad to hear some of your gripes as well, not that I necessarily agree with how you blame me for them. Still, it gives me a sense that you too are invested in doing something different in the future." For others, however, the opening of this door can be deeply threatening and uncomfortable. "I am not used to talking about my discomfort. I just put down my head and barrel through, and usually things come out all right or I move on. When there's a problem I seek to solve it; I don't like having to discuss my feelings and deepest concerns. I feel exposed and vulnerable in a way that may make me run in the opposite direction." Both reactions might occur in the same setting. The job of the facilitator is to work with both driving and restraining forces. A plan for change must include addressing and if possible alleviating legitimate fears and resistances. Those who seek to drive the process forward may be empowered to foster confidence in those resisting it, articulating that it need not be as threatening or painful as they fear. In the meantime the intervention may need to be suspended while internal motivation and confidence are fostered, usually among those resisting. (It is helpful to summarize the results of a conflict audit, as shown in Exhibit 8.1.)

In the church case the surfacing of the conflict leads to important insights and renewal. A parishioner says, "Please know, Reverend Donalds, that you are very important to us, and we do not want to lose you or your respect for us. It is important to us that you not view those opposing your proposal as mean-spirited; rather, we are fearful. Recognizing our concerns for quality of life and safety in our neighborhoods, we wonder if there might not be other ways we can contribute to alleviating the plight of the homeless."

This leads to the establishment of a committee charged to study the issue of homelessness in general and to educate the community. Another group is charged with proposing a series of alternative options for responding most appropriately to this issue as a community. In the end the community agrees to begin with a food and clothing drive. This evolves into a "meals for a friend" program, where members cook meals in the church and deliver them to

Exhibit 8.1. Conflict Audit of Church Dispute.

Conflict Audit Summary Sheet

Identity Issues	Interests	Driving Forces	Restraining Forces
Church mission	Food and	Strong	Fear that
Leadership	shelter for	leadership	addressing
values	homeless	Engagement in	issue will
Community	Church and	community	be more
safety	community	over issue	divisive than
Unity in	resources		ignoring it
church and			Previous
community			attempts to
			discuss issue
			led to deep
			divisions

homeless shelters. Finally, it grows into a dynamic program in which church members "adopt" homeless families and help them, with church resources, get back on their feet.

Employing the ARIA Framework: A Brief Road Map (a prototypical two-day workshop)

The town of Willings, Idaho, a long-time farming community, was faced with an influx of Californians who were fleeing city life and seeking a return to simpler ways. A serious conflict, somewhat paradoxical in nature, arose when the already established community wanted rapid development, from interstate highways to Wal-Marts—the modern "conveniences" from which the newer community had just fled. Community leaders planned a two-day session to address the conflict.

Using this situation as an example, the ARIA process will be illustrated in a step-by-step fashion following the route in Figure 8.2.

Antagonism (approximately two hours)

What are the problems at stake in this conflict? What is it about?

This is a deceptively simple question, but because most people in a difficult conflict will automatically frame it in adversarial ways, this question usually opens up the kind of blaming, polarization, attributions, and projection typical of an antagonistic discussion.

"They say they want charm," exclaim the older residents. "We know what it's like to drive fifteen miles on back roads to get our children to the doctor's office." The newer residents retort, "You want a Wal-Mart and the conveniences of the modern era because you haven't experienced the dislocation, drugs, violence, and crime that accompany this kind of faceless development."

In what ways do you blame others for the problem? Be specific.

"They come with their fancy cars, money for all conveniences,

Figure 8.2. The Road Map to Reconciliation.

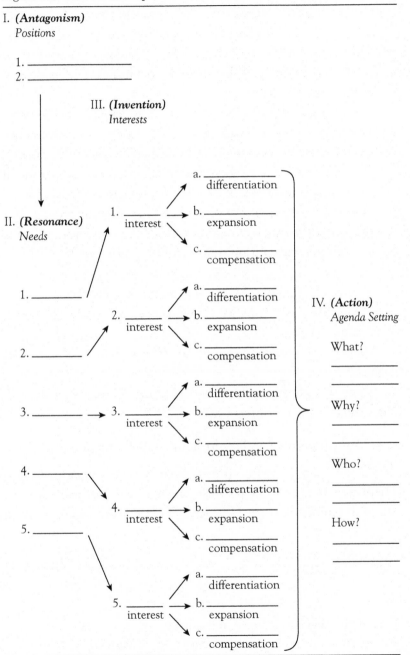

and foolish ideas about the simple life—like the way we hang our laundry on lines in our back yards. We're sick of their self-righteous, holier-than-thou attitudes. Simply put, they are spoiled, rich kids who don't know what hard work is like. If they want to wash their clothes by hand, they're welcome to do so, but just don't expect us to do it if we can find any way around it."

The other side responds, "Speaking of romanticism, they have naive and uninformed notions about modern life. Along with convenience comes emptiness. We know; we've been there. They watch the rich on television and fantasize about the good life, confident that moral depravity won't taint them. It will. In fact, it seems it already has!"

After the right amount of this antagonistic framing process (not too little, not too much), facilitators take the temperature of the groups with the expectation that it will be a bit feverish.

How are you feeling now? What do you think about this process?

"Awful. How is this helping? We've been after each other this way for quite a while."

"Why are you making us recite all of this again?! Let's just call it quits."

When this step has gone far enough the facilitators may want to chart the group's positions (Exhibit 8.2).

Resonance (approximately four hours—likely finishing the first day)

There are two ways to help parties move from antagonism to resonance. If tempers flare or if intragroup tensions are considerable, a

Exhibit 8.2. Positions.

Antagonism

Positions
1. Promote rapid development and growth
2. Restrict development; keep community simple and small

---

two-step process of caucusing in separate groups and doing a reflex-ive reframing exercise is useful. The other approach skips caucus-ing and is appropriate for disputants who seem ripe for a more direct and immediately interactive reframing process.

Step One: Intragroup Reframing. Disputants are separated into opposing sides and invited to sit around a flip chart on which their PNIs (positions, needs, and interests) are listed. If a group has only one position (perhaps that *all* types of development should be held to a minimum), they stay around the chart and work as a single unit. If they have more than one substantive position on their own side—an intergroup conflict of sorts—they break into as many groups as they have positions (for example, that only *some* types of development be restricted). It is actually useful if there is intragroup diversity around positions because this gives a group some "prac-tice" within their own side, going through the same process they will soon go through with their adversaries. For each position a group has, they generate a number of underlying needs such as for identity, dignity, and so forth. For each need identified, groups artic-ulate several interests (or means) by which those needs might be fulfilled, such as cultural expression, recognition, security measures, and so forth.

The process to be followed is much the same regardless of whether these discussions are taking place between entire groups or in subgroups. First, articulate the whys (needs, values, motivations) that lie beneath the group's position. Discuss why they matter so much. Illustrate and concretize with examples, when possible, to give the words life. For instance, parties will ask themselves, "Why do we care so much about making sure there's no development of any kind?" When someone responds, "Because we have seen what devel-opment does to the human spirit," someone else (probably a person designated as group facilitator) will seek to probe further and ask, "What exactly does it do? What do you seek or fear?" Someone else responds, "We fear that life becomes superficial and meaningless."

Summarizing the needs and values at stake, the facilitator might ask, "So you seek meaning?" The underlying motivation is clear when a questioner no longer has to ask for further analysis or explanation, when it is evident that the human dimension—the underlying need or value rather than positions or interests—has been articulated (Exhibit 8.3).

Having expressed the needs that lie beneath their positions, the groups then begin the process of translating needs into functional interests. For each need expressed, participants are encouraged to generate several possible interests or means of fulfilling those needs (Figure 8.3).[2]

Step Two: Intergroup Reframing. The separate groups now come back together. Setting aside the positions previously separating them, they begin an exploration of their respective and shared needs. The facilitator sets the stage and asks a few questions to get the reframing process going. I find it helpful to begin by pointing out that in previous sessions, with a focus on positions, we had an antagonistic

Exhibit 8.3. Needs.

Resonance

Position 1: Promote rapid development and growth
Needs
1. Safety
2. Well-being
3. Self-respect
4. Control

Resonance

Position 2: Restrict development; keep community simple and small
Needs
1. Meaning
2. Safety
3. Control

Figure 8.3. Developing Interests.

Position 1: Promote rapid development and growth

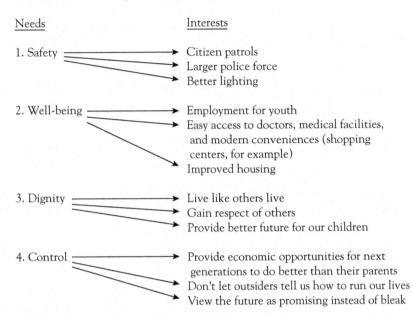

Needs

1. Safety

2. Well-being

3. Dignity

4. Control

Interests

Citizen patrols
Larger police force
Better lighting

Employment for youth
Easy access to doctors, medical facilities,
   and modern conveniences (shopping
   centers, for example)
Improved housing

Live like others live
Gain respect of others
Provide better future for our children

Provide economic opportunities for next
   generations to do better than their parents
Don't let outsiders tell us how to run our lives
View the future as promising instead of bleak

Position 2: Restrict development and keep community simple and small

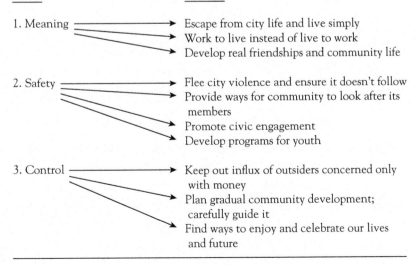

Needs

1. Meaning

2. Safety

3. Control

Interests

Escape from city life and live simply
Work to live instead of live to work
Develop real friendships and community life

Flee city violence and ensure it doesn't follow
Provide ways for community to look after its
   members
Promote civic engagement
Develop programs for youth

Keep out influx of outsiders concerned only
   with money
Plan gradual community development;
   carefully guide it
Find ways to enjoy and celebrate our lives
   and future

discussion that left us all deeply dissatisfied and frustrated. I urge participants to try a new kind of discourse, one in which they are interactively introspective about what is motivating this conflict— what they care about so much and why—and what their hopes and fears are regarding those motivations. I ask someone to pick one of the needs their group said was motivating its positions (and thus the conflict). This person explains to the other side why this need is so important to their group, why it matters so much, and what hopes and fears are tied into this need in connection with this conflict.

For example, around the need for dignity, one might hear, "We need to feel respected and intelligent. With all those urban intellectuals coming in, we feel dull and humiliated." On the issue of control, "We need to feel greater control over our lives and destinies. Living in cities, we have felt battered by external forces that controlled us. We want a different life."

This leads to the construction of a single list of underlying needs and motivations (Exhibit 8.4). Although they may not have listed identical needs, groups always find shared needs and motivations through their conversations. Discussion may also lead to the articulation of a statement of shared concerns such as, "We citizens of Willings, long-time and newly arrived, seek to foster a community that fulfills our shared and respective needs for dignity, meaning, safety, and control over our destiny. We believe that by working together, we can develop our shared home together in this way." It is becoming clear to both sides that their conflict is motivated by similar needs, and there is momentum to move forward.

Integrative Inventing (approximately two hours)

Having made explicit the kinds of underlying needs and values that must be fulfilled for any solutions to be effective, the sides now work in mixed teams to develop inventions. The first step is to negotiate combinations of their respective interests, as shown in Exhibit 8.5.

Having agreed to shared interests, now the sides form mixed working groups (constituted of members from both sides) and seek

Exhibit 8.4. Shared Needs.

Shared Needs
1. Safety
2. Dignity
3. Meaning
4. Control
5. Well-being

to generate inventions. In this process, participants are constantly reality-testing their ideas against the criteria established by the needs and values articulated during reflexive discourse. Though not wholly nonevaluative, as is the case with classical brainstorming, it nonetheless should be conducted so that expansive and imaginative ideas are considered. The inventing process is a kind of guided creativity.

Criteria for "good inventions" have already been outlined in the mutually acceptable shared needs and values described during reflexive reframing. They were further explicated during discussions about the needs and values at stake for each side and again while articulating shared needs. (However, needs are no longer lined up with specific interests; all the needs are viewed as criteria for evaluating all inventions.) Thus as mixed teams work to fully develop the inventions, they stay true to the essential needs and values.

It is once again helpful to use the techniques for generating integrative solutions discussed in Chapter Four: differentiation, expansion, and compensation.

Differentiation. When interests appear to be valued differently, parties can try to build integrative solutions through differentiation techniques. (For example, when only one orange is available for two people, they may discover that one person wants it for the juice and the other for baking. They decide to divide it; one gets the fruit and one the peel.)

Exhibit 8.5. Negotiating Combined Interests.

Interests of Group One:	Interests of Group Two:	Negotiated Combinations
Citizen patrols	Escape from city and	Develop joint council
Employment for	live simply	to plan for
youth	Develop real	community
Easy access to doctors,	friendships and	involvement in
medical facilities,	community life	promoting safety
and modern	Flee city violence and	(citizen patrols
conveniences	ensure it doesn't	and so on)
(shopping centers,	follow	Develop
for example)	Provide ways for	opportunities for
Improved housing	community to look	voluntary activities
Live like others live	after its members	to improve
Provide better future	Promote civic	community, while
for our children	engagement	promoting civic
Provide economic	Develop programs for	connections
opportunities for	youth	Develop local
next generations	Keep out influx of	employment
to do better than	outsiders concerned	opportunities that
their parents	only with money	do not require
Don't let outsiders	Plan gradual	outside chains
tell us how to run	community	(like Wal-Marts)
our lives	development;	Plan educational
View the future as	carefully guide it	programs in which
promising instead	Find ways to enjoy	new and long-time
of bleak	and celebrate our	residents learn
	lives and future	about each other
		Bring in outside
		community
		development
		professionals to
		help citizens guide
		growth to meet the
		needs of all citizens
		most fully

Expansion. Using expansion techniques, parties attempt to expand the amount, type, and use of available resources. Parties can develop more of an existing resource, they can add different types of resources, and they can foster a new way to use an existing resource. (For example, when only one orange is available for two people, they might explore ways to locate another orange.)

Compensation. Using compensation techniques, parties must first determine the extent to which they prioritize their interests differently from one another. They can attempt to offer exchanges or compensation for differently valued issues and interests. (When only one orange is available for two people, they may discover that they prioritize the value of the orange differently. They may then decide that one person will get the orange and pay compensation to the other.)

Exhibit 8.6 presents an example of how the group dealing with safety needs moves to shared interests and on to inventions.

Action Planning (approximately two hours)

With outlines of the various invention ideas posted on pieces of paper around the room, the group now makes decisions about the level, scale, and type of their next steps. Stepping back and looking over the A-R-I steps that have been taken to this point, they review their initial and opposing positions regarding growth. They also take note of how they have reframed the conflict in terms of community development, planned and paced in such a way as to satisfy the basic needs of all the residents of Willings—for dignity, control over destiny, and high quality of life. Agreeing that the reframe will provide the foundation for healthy development, they then review their various inventions and ask, What is to be done? Why? How? and By whom? They decide to start with a single initiative around safety issues, hoping that it will foster confidence and momentum for further cooperation and problem solving.

Exhibit 8.6. Inventions for Safety Needs.

Needs:	*Interests*:	*Inventions*:
Safety	Develop joint citizen council	*Differentiation:* Each group has different experience with safety issues. They plan educational programs to learn about each other's experiences, hopes, and fears.
		Expansion: While community lacks resources for an expanded police force, with a new tax base more funds will be available. However, use of these funds should be explored. Perhaps citizen patrol groups, conflict resolution training in schools, and even a local mediation program could be launched with new resources and greater civic engagement.
		Compensation: Exchanges can be made with other work groups. For example, for the new residents, safety concerns are primary; for the older residents, economic development is their key concern. Thus groups can agree to support each other's efforts and seek to identify with their concerns.

Action Planning Worksheet

1. *Task Statement* (What?). Develop a specific project proposal for each intergroup (joint, coordinated, or parallel) peace-building initiative (invention) designed to address shared problems.

A community safety task force is established to launch educational programs and study the need for and feasibility of citizen patrols.

2. *Objective Statement* (Why?). Which needs will be addressed by each initiative and in what ways?

Ensuring that safety concerns of the residents can be met in conjunction with community building.

3. *Participants and Activities* (Who?). Describe who will do what to achieve objectives.

A balanced group of volunteers and community leaders from both sectors (new and long-term residents) will serve on the task force. It will be co-chaired by representatives from both sectors of the community.

4. *Modalities* (How?). Describe the human, financial, and organizational structures and resources necessary to successfully implement each initiative.

The task force will be set up within a month and serve an initial term of twelve months. Most meetings will be open to public observation and input. Meetings will be held in the teachers' lounge of the local high school. Funds for light refreshments and for small initiatives the committee may want to launch (uniforms for citizen patrol members, flashlights, for example) will be drawn from a new community chest fund to be developed in conjunction with this task force.

5. *Resistance*. What forces will constrain, slow down, or stop the efforts?

Rejectionists on both side of the divide. People who are afraid; people who lack confidence in their own voice and efficacy.

6. *Support.* What forces will support, speed up, or help promote the efforts?

Clear communication to the community about task force purposes and plans. The editor of the local newspaper has expressed great interest in this effort and promises to regularly and constructively report on it to the community. Town meetings are also planned on a quarterly basis to report on the work of the task force.

Conclusion

I hope this chapter has helped further bring to life applications of the ARIA framework. As the process has evolved over the past decade, I have tried to synthesize some of the best theories and practices in the field in a straightforward and user-friendly way. The examples given in this and earlier chapters have demonstrated that ARIA can be adapted and applied in many different settings. Certain aspects of ARIA may be useful in a particular conflict, others not. I fully expect that practitioners will pick and choose selectively to suit their needs. I would like to hear from people who use the framework in whole or in parts, whether they are professional analysts, third parties, or participants in a conflict intervention. ARIA is most certainly a work in progress, and feedback will help shape its refinement and further evolution. ARIA will grow and succeed most fully when those singing its song can make their own music.

Epilogue

* *

Engaging Identity, Creating Harmony

As I was completing the manuscript for this book I came across an article in the *New Yorker* profiling the Orpheus Ensemble. This exceptional group leads itself, without using a conductor, and has developed a reputation for true resonance within each musician and between them (Traub, 1996).

I was immediately struck by the parallels between the Orpheus Ensemble and the fictional quartet I have created here to illustrate the ARIA framework. The musicians seemed to be describing the very act of conflict engagement: "When you play in an ordinary orchestra, there's a clear limit to your responsibility. You're expected to show up and play well and do what the conductor says. It's a lot like typing. Everybody is afraid to question the conductor. People develop these tremendous conflicts to the point where they can barely speak to each other. We're always fighting with each other, but we're always fighting it *out*" (p. 103).

Although the Orpheus Ensemble does not follow the ARIA script per se, the group apparently has discovered ways to transform their fights and antagonism into constructive engagement and resonance. One pianist who frequently plays with the Orpheus Ensemble says with awe that he can hardly understand how the musicians play so unfailingly together. But he suspects the answer "lies in the musician's sense of trust, the intensity with which they listen to one another and the responsibility that each player takes for the entire score, and not just his own part. And this process of adjustment and meshing occurs not only among the musicians but between the whole group and the soloist as well" (p. 104).

Life imitates art imitates life.

Notes

· ·

Chapter One

1. In this book I am concerned with identity primarily as it is
   expressed in the context of groups. Group identity is defined and
   viewed through many different disciplinary lenses. Writings about
   ethnonational conflicts have proliferated along with the rise of such
   conflicts on the world scene in the latter part of this century; both
   political scientists and social psychologists refer to them as "collective conflicts" (Connor, 1994; Smith, 1986, 1991; Rouhana, 1997).
   A prominent theory in social psychology, "social identity theory"
   (Tajfel, 1981), is concerned with primary group affiliations and
   social relations that individuals choose or maintain. Psychologists
   such as Erikson view identity as the sum-total of "self," or the
   integration of an individual's various primary affiliations (Erikson,
   1950). As Rouhana suggests, "Further exploration of the relationships among collective identity, social identity, and personal identity is needed." In the meantime, whether these distinctions are
   viewed as relatively arbitrary, with individual and social identity
   complexly interwoven (Deaux, 1992), or usefully disaggregated
   (Hogg and Abrams, 1988), it is safe to assert that groups clearly
   serve to provide individuals with meaningful affiliation, security,
   recognition, and purpose. Here I employ the notion of group
   identity somewhat metaphorically—as a "corporate individual"
   itself requiring security, recognition, and so forth. (In fact, it is

the individuals within groups whose needs are fulfilled or expressed through group affiliation and loyalty.)

2. Moving between levels of analysis has important implications for both theory building and practice. Theoretically, Etzioni (1968, pp. 358–601) presents four justifications for analogical borrowing from lower levels to higher levels of analysis (individual to international relations): pragmatic reasons (it offers insight); heuristic needs (it may help in formulation of new propositions); logical validity (it makes sense); and theoretical validity (there is internal consistency across levels). Practically, Deutsch (1973) asserts that not only may one speak in the same terms about conflict at different levels—intrapsychic, interpersonal, intergroup, and international—but that it is useful to do so. He writes that general principles can be used to characterize conflict and conflict resolution that are applicable across various levels. Boulding was even bolder in his suggestion that there is a general phenomenon of conflict, and he sought to provide a general theory of conflict that applies to all areas of human life and organization (1962). Kahn and Zald (1990, p. 398) self-consciously look for analogies across organizational and national levels of analysis when they suggest, "The welcome movement toward more open and peaceful relations among nations brings international and organizational issues more closely together." If, as this book posits, identity conflict as a class of conflict readily moves across levels of social organization, it will be a further tool in analogical and comparative analysis, as well as an aid to decision making about appropriate means and timing for intervention. Having said all that, I want to offer a caution about overgeneralization, along with other theorists who suggest that though there is a general category of phenomena that share similar conflict characteristics, "conflicts of individuals and groups, organizations and nation-states require explanations that take account of their emergent differences as well as their similarities" (Katz and Kahn, 1966, p. 612). Thus although I assert that identity conflict is a ubiquitous form of conflict across different levels of social organization, it is manifested in different ways requiring theoretical and applied flexibility. However, as I am developing a general and applied model

in this book, I am overemphasizing similarities and perhaps under-emphasizing differences.

3. In the last twenty years a significant trend in the field of international relations has focused on identity groups and the threats and frustrations to their needs for "security, distinctive identity, social recognition of identity, and effective participation in the processes that determine conditions of security and identity" (Azar, 1990, p. 29). Instead of emphasizing competition between nation states over their "national interests," as does the classical approach to international relations (Morgenthau, 1948), this approach views group identity needs within and between nation-states as a crucial unit of analysis in determining international war or peace. This has led to research and conflict intervention focusing on the ways such identity needs can be expressed and reconciled to begin reversing a cycle of violence and conflict intractability (Burton, 1979; Kriesberg, Northrup, and Thorson, 1989; Kelman, 1993; Mitchell and Banks, 1996; Rothman, 1992). Also, devoting a considerable amount of energy and attention to the study of identity groups in politics and conflict, a field of political psychology—a hybrid discipline of social psychology and politics has been emerging over the last several decades with its own professional association, journal, and college courses dedicated to this topic.

4. By the middle of the twentieth century, labor relations began to outgrow its purely adversarial origins born of unfair and exploitative management practices and the development of the labor movement in reaction to them. Thus the study and practice of industrial relations was born, along with such institutions as the U.S. National Labor Relations Board (NLRB), with mandates to find ways to forge more cooperative relations and modes of problem solving and collective bargaining. In the early part of this century Mary Parker Follet was writing about "integrative bargaining" in organizations to replace domination or compromise, both of which she viewed as dysfunctional to effective organizational life (Follet, 1941). It was increasingly suggested that organizations must be as concerned with the human dimension and quality of work life as with their output and production (McGregor, 1960). Although previously the

organizational system and bureaucracy (Weber, 1947) and a "science of management" (Taylor, 1911) were nearly exclusively emphasized in organization theory and practice, a psychodynamic or humanistic interpretation of persons in organizational life began to be viewed as central to its effectiveness, as well as one of its central purposes (Bion, 1961). Affiliation and the desire to be accepted by one's group were shown to significantly influence collaborative or competitive behavior between managers and stewards (Stagner and Rosen, 1965). Beginning in the 1960s scholars and organizational consultants like Blake, Shepard, and Mouton (1964); Walton and McKersie (1966); Likert and Likert (1976); Thomas (1976); Brown (1983); Tjosvold (1992); and Bazerman and Lewicki (1983) built on this human relations approach to organizational life to promote collaborative, integrative approaches to management and labor and industrial relations.

5. A very brief bibliographic excursion here into the history of the conflict management and resolution fields and the different terminologies and procedures they use will be useful to place myself and position the approach and language—conflict engagement—emphasized in this book. Built in significant measure upon the evolution in labor and industrial relations described in the Note #4, a wider field of interest-based conflict management evolved in some ways as an alternative to legalistic and litigious means of addressing disputes (for a good review of the "alternative dispute resolution" (ADR) movement see Carbonneau, 1989). Its most popular incarnation was in "Principled Bargaining," which was launched most fully in the early 1980s by theorists and practitioners at or affiliated to Harvard University and later sustained and promoted primarily by the Harvard-based Program on Negotiation, and widely applied to law, diplomacy, environmental disputes and business (see Fisher and Ury, 1981; Susskind and Cruikshank, 1987; Pruitt and Rubin, 1986; Raifa, 1982; Goldberg, Green, and Sander, 1985; Moore, 1986).

At about the same time and focused primarily on diplomacy, building on the small-group dynamics movement (Lewin, 1948) and a new view of cybernetics or self-steering and internal feedback systems of decision making in international relations (Deutsch, 1963), a new "global politics" approach was taking shape to replace the static power-politics model that emphasized the role of human needs in international conflict and conflict resolution (Banks, 1984). This approach, also known as the analytical (or interactive) problem-solving approach, views conflict as a result of threatened or frustrated needs that must be surfaced, fully analyzed and addressed, at least in principle, before any kind of bargaining, settlement, or negotiation can succeed (Burton, 1979; Kelman, 1982; Azar, 1990).

Finally in the early 1990s, some theorist-practitioners at both international and community levels (notably Lederach, 1995; Rupesinghe, 1995; Folger and Bush, 1995) found both sets of frameworks and terms—management and resolution—lacking. They suggested that instead of seeking to manage conflicts, implying that they are negative problems to be ameliorated, conflicts should be viewed as positive opportunities for growth and moral development, to be embraced and transformed. "A conflict confronts each party with a challenge, a difficulty, or adversity to be grappled with. This challenge presents parties with the opportunity to clarify for themselves their needs and values, what causes them dissatisfaction and satisfaction" (Folger and Bush, 1995, p. 82). Even needs theorists suggest that conflict is not a final state but rather a dynamic process likened to the progressive peeling of an onion, wherein as one problem is solved, a new one emerges in need of resolution. Thus instead of seeking to resolve conflicts, these theorist-practitioners suggest that conflicts are to be embraced and mined for their creative and transformational potentials. The philosophy of this "school" is captured by the Chinese character for "crisis," which simultaneously means "opportunity."

In addition it is useful to note that somewhat in parallel to the "transformation" school, but mostly detached from it and the conflict resolution movement generally, another school, perhaps best labeled the "dialogue" school has been emerging in the past decade or so that has much relevance to the field and my own work (see Bohm, 1980; Senge, 1990; Isaacs, 1993; Jones, 1996; Becker and others, 1995). This school, or at least my connection to it, is based on many theoretical foundations including theology, phenomenology, critical theory, and constructivism (Buber, 1937; Goffman,

1950; Bateson, 1972; Mehan and Wood, 1975; Habermas, 1979; Argyris, Putnam, and Smith, 1985).

6. The field of conflict studies and intervention has grown rapidly over the past thirty years as reviewed earlier. The terminology used, the definition of success (see Ross and Rothman, forthcoming) and its applications vary widely. Even the use of the primary terms—conflict management, resolution, transformation—mean different things to different theorists and practitioners. Given all this fluidity, I am fairly agnostic about the "best" approach, believing that it is essentially a question of specificity of conflict type, stage, and sequence that should determine which set of definitions, theories and methods are most appropriate and when. As will be seen, the ARIA framework builds on each of these theoretical and practical streams in the evolving field of conflict study and intervention.

However, having stated my agnosticism it is still useful to place my work and training in context of the above review of the emerging field and its various streams. As noted in the Preface, my work in this field was first inspired by the works of Martin Buber (1937), Horace Kallen (1956), and Martin Luther King, Jr. (1967). Entering graduate school, I was taught by some of the key leaders in the international conflict resolution school (most notably Azar, 1990; Burton, 1979; and Kelman, 1982). Simultaneous to that training I also studied small-group dynamics and organization development, especially at the National Training Laboratories (NTL) (see Benne and others, 1975; Schein and Bennis, 1965) and from the consulting and training firm, Interaction Associates (see Doyle and Strauss, 1976).

Although I have incorporated key aspects of the "interest-based" approaches to conflict management in my work, I think it has too often attempted to "manage" identity-based conflicts in ways that are unhelpful and sequentially or temporally inappropriate. Here, proper analysis, sequencing, and timing are of the essence (see Kriesberg and Thorson, 1991). I firmly believe that only when identity concerns are surfaced through the kind of analytical process promoted by the conflict resolution and dialogue schools, and perhaps somewhat transformed as vehicles for moral and general development, can they be "ripe" for interest-based conflict management. On the other hand (distinct from some who feel resolution, dialogue, or transformation are the end of the process), I believe that at the later stage of conflict processing or engagement, interest-based bargaining or conflict management has much to offer by way of concretization and consolidation.

Throughout this book I use many of the terms in the field somewhat interchangeably because, as is appropriate for this relatively new field, they are so widely and variously used. However, I also use the terms "conflict processing" and "engagement" both to get away from, and where useful synthesize, the specific theoretical and applied meanings, such as they are, of conflict management, resolution, dialogue, or transformation.

7. Ross (1993a) suggests that intransigent conflict results from a complex interplay between psychocultural dynamics and interpretations and substantive "interests." Azar (1990) also describes how frustrated human needs and competition over scarce resources negatively reinforce each other. Both suggest that although substantive interest conflicts, such as those over resources and inequality, directly contribute to forging or sustaining deep identity conflicts, to ameliorate them, underlying needs must often be first addressed and emphasized.

Chapter Two

1. Polyani (1966); Watzlawicki, Wakland, and Fisch (1974), Schön (1983) and Schön and Rein (1994) all suggest that in order to engage in a successful change process of any kind, which explicitly or implicitly includes any conflict-resolution process, the point of departure (the "tacit" assumptions or the original frames defining the focus of attention) must first be made explicit. As Schön writes, "When we set the problem, we select what we will treat as the 'things' of the situation, we set the boundaries of our attentions to it, and we impose upon it a coherence which allows us to say what is wrong and in what directions the situation needs to be changed. Problem setting is a process in which, interactively, we *name* the things to which we will attend and *frame* the context in which we will attend to them." (1983, p. 40)

2. Attribution theory has been both theoretically (Jones and others, 1972) and experimentally (Sillars, 1981) developed primarily in social psychology. It has been frequently applied to conflict theory and resolution (Fisher, 1990). In an experiment with college roommates, Sillars demonstrated how those who attributed negative disposition to their roommates escalated conflict, while those who accepted at least some measure of responsibility for daily or exceptional conflicts reduced their intensity or damage to the relationship.

Chapter Three

1. The idea of viewing identity formation and expression as a function of narrative and storytelling is built on a rich literature (Charme, 1984; Sarbin, 1986; Bruner, 1987; Smith, 1986; Derringer, 1991). It can also provide a fertile basis for a reflexive approach to conflict resolution, which elicits and guides interactive storytelling between groups in conflict as a tool for moving them from dissonance to resonance.

2. From a Jewish New Year's message produced by the Jewish Theological Seminary, 1988.

3. On a less metaphysical plane, there is an extensive literature on how disputants convince one another to cooperate for mutual gains. Game theory and the idea of tit-for-tat (including positive behavior) is one such literature (see Axelrod, 1984). In international relations, building on this notion of inducing adversaries to behave cooperatively, an early theory applied to nuclear disarmament was the notion of GRIT ("gradual reduction of international tension") through sequenced acts of cooperation and confidence building (Osgood, 1962).

4. Clearly, one concern about such unilateral change is what to do with an adversary who does not engage in this open process. Can you tango without a partner? The answer is a qualified yes. Going to the dance floor and inviting a partner on, even when he or she is unwilling and ultimately refuses, can foster dynamics that may lead to a willingness to dance later. In a conflict situation it can change the game and dynamics positively, even if only one party is open and publicly introspective. Nevertheless, the degree of transformative potential is by definition limited. Moreover, if it is not recipro-

cal, at least at some point (which may come later if not at the beginning), then it is not clear whether true reflexivity can occur.

5. Power disequilibrium is an important and complex topic that merits and receives serious consideration in conflict studies (see Rouhana and Fiske, 1995; Duke, 1976; and Boulding, 1989). I am not addressing it here. Instead, I am furthering a useful distinction about the notion of power *with* others to cooperatively accomplish something inclusive, instead of power *over* others to unilaterally achieve something exclusive.

6. It is useful to note that the specific human needs that various theorists write about and practitioners seek to promote range widely in concept if not so much in practice. In his *Social Contract*, Rousseau (1893) spoke of the rights of man, and this became the key concept of the French Revolution. President Woodrow Wilson spoke of "self-determination," and this became the byword of the League of Nations. Ted Robert Gurr (1970) writes of welfare values, power values, and interpersonal values. Paul Sites (1973), from whom Burton derived his specific theory of the role of human needs in international conflict, discusses needs for response and consistency in response, stimulation, security, recognition, distributive justice, the need to appear rational, and to develop rationality, meaning, and control. Pruitt and Rubin (1986) discuss needs for security, identity, social approval, happiness, clarity about the nature of one's world, and physical well-being. Galtung (1990) discusses security, freedom, welfare, and identity as the key human needs. While most theorists writing about needs in international relations hold that people have all needs simultaneously (both physiological and psychological), Abraham Maslow suggests a hierarchy of needs. As noted earlier, he suggests that people must first achieve basic needs like physiological maintenance, safety and security and then may begin moving up the ladder to fulfill needs for love and belongingness, self-esteem, and ultimately for self-actualization. Finally, it is worth pointing out that theorists also argue over what are basic needs and what are instrumental needs. Sites suggests, for instance, that what some call needs for freedom and belonging are actually instrumental, or necessary conditions, for the fulfillment of essential needs (1990, p. 24).

Chapter Four

1. Fisher and Ury suggest that "needs are the most essential of interests" (1981, p. 49). Moore suggests that interests can be viewed in multiple ways: substantive interests, procedural interests, and psychological interests (1986, p. 37). There is merit to this broad and inclusive view of interests; but part of the claim of this book is that we need to begin distinguishing types of conflicts in part so that we can develop clear criteria for selecting forms of intervention. Therefore, I believe separating out the human dimension—needs—from resource and functional aspects of conflicts—interests—is useful in evolving greater conceptual and practical clarity.

2. To guard against naive optimism that real conflicts can ever have fully win-win outcomes, Lax and Sabenius (1986) in *The Manager as Negotiator: Bargaining for Cooperation and Competitive Gains* write, "As a full conception of negotiation, the 'win-win philosophy' is misleading and wrong. Even if two negotiators were fully open about their preferences, honest, and creative, they would not eliminate the distributive element of their bargain. In fact, they might enhance its salience" (p. 156). Conversely, as the authors point out, viewing conflicts as solely distributive misses an important window of opportunity to find and invent areas for cooperation and mutual gain between disputants.

3. For further discussions of what is variously called integration, integrative bargaining, and integrative problem solving, see Walton and McKersie (1965) and Lewicki and Litterer (1985). Pruitt and Rubin (1986, pp. 143–148) speak of five types of integrative procedures: expanding the pie, nonspecific compensation, logrolling, cost-cutting, and bridging. The concept of integrative problem solving shares much in common with Muzafer Sherif's concept of "superordinate goals" (1961). As described previously, in this approach parties in conflict articulate existing goals or structure new goals that each party wants separately but can only gain through cooperation with the other side. For example, rival groups in a summer camp bond together to pull a food delivery truck out of the mud so they may have dinner that evening.

In an essay by Stephen P. Cohen and Harriet Arnone (1988), "Conflict Resolution as the Alternative to Terrorism," without using the term the authors suggest integrative strategies for addressing the Arab-Israeli conflict. They suggest five steps: enhancement of each adversary's identity, creation of new symbols, enfranchisement of elements within each group (to support a peace process), enhancement of indigenous development (as a benefit of peace), and use of indigenous third parties. Thus outcomes are sought in which parties' own positions are improved without any decrease for the other side. In fact, the gains on both sides become mutually enforcing.

Chapter Five

1. In 1991, shortly after the historic Middle East Peace Conference held in Madrid under joint U.S. and Russian sponsorship, Israelis and Palestinians were into their eighth round of relatively fruitless discussions at the offices of the U.S. State Department. Meeting with one of the high-level organizers of these meetings, I asked why he was planning a ninth meeting instead of searching for a new agenda. He responded that the job at hand was simply to keep the parties talking—to maintain the negotiation process—until "willy nilly," some breakthrough occurred. It finally did occur, about a year later, but only when a secret set of negotiations in Oslo between Israeli academics and PLO representatives reached common ground on a new substantive basis for proceeding.

2. In their essay "Toward a Theory of Agenda Setting in Negotiations," Balakrishnan, Patton, and Lewis (1993) retell the following story: "After a reverse in Napoleon's fortunes, L'Empereur stated that he felt it was necessary to win another battle quickly before allowing his foreign minister, Talleyrand, to attend an (already planned) conference with the opposing allies. Talleyrand gently pointed out to Napoleon that winning another battle was not really necessary before the meeting. The reason he gave was recorded by his secretary as follows: 'Sire, it is not necessary. They have allowed me to set the agenda'" (Woosley, 1991, p. 105).

Chapter Six

1. When running intercommunal workshops such as those between Jews and Arabs, it is important that the facilitation team be carefully

constructed. Because I am Jewish, I run such workshops with Arab colleagues. My main cofacilitators in these workshops were Amal Jamal and Mohammed Dawarshe.

2. Robin Twite, project coordinator, conceptualized and drafted much of this statement.

Chapter Seven

1. Adapted from an instrument developed by Tod Colbert, president, Weather Tight Corporation. Anecdote of its successful use also told by him.

Chapter Eight

1. There is a real danger of launching a conflict transformation process if solid commitment is lacking to devote all necessary resources (usually time and money) to see the process through. I have had several unfortunate experiences when individuals or groups have withdrawn from the process with antagonism surfaced and nerves frayed. Third parties must endeavor to build commitment among participants for a whole process before embarking on it, explaining that early stages may be quite painful. (There is, however, an unfortunate reality that explanations and warnings don't always suffice, and aborted interventions may occur despite vigilance and best intentions.)

2. If there is more than one list generated by each group (if they have more than one position), they will have to negotiate and integrate a common list to bring back to the table. After each subgroup has fully conceptualized their needs and interests, they then come back to the others on their side and present their plans for the merging and meshing of needs and interests. After transferring the same or very similar needs and interests from both lists, some intragroup negotiation takes place where needs and interests substantially differ. Once a consensus is reached that those needs and interests represent all voices from one side, they are put on a final joint list, and the group is ready for interactive introspection with the other side.

References

Argyris, C., Putnam, R., and Smith, D. M. *Action Science: Concepts, Methods, and Skills for Research and Intervention*. San Francisco: Jossey-Bass, 1985.

Argyris, C., and Schön, D. *Organizational Learning: A Theory of Action Perspective*. Reading, Mass.: Addison-Wesley, 1978.

Axelrod, R. *The Evolution of Cooperation*. New York: Basic Books, 1984.

Azar, E. "Protracted Social Conflicts: Ten Propositions." In E. Azar and J. Burton (eds.), *International Conflict Resolution: Theory and Practice*. Aldershot, England: Dartmouth, 1986.

Azar, E. *The Management of Protracted Social Conflict: Theory and Cases*. Aldershot, England: Dartmouth, 1990.

Baker, J., Remarks at Royal Palace, Madrid, Nov. 1, 1991. From U.S. Department of State Dispatch, November 4, 1991, p. 809.

Balakrishnan, P. V., Patton, C., and Lewis, P. "Toward a Theory of Agenda Setting in Negotiations." *Journal of Consumer Affairs*, Mar. 1993, 19, 637–654.

Banks, M. (ed.). *Conflict in World Society: A New Perspective on International Relations*. Sussex: Wheatsheaf Books, 1984.

Bateson, G. *Steps to an Ecology of Mind*. New York: Chandler, 1972.

Bazerman, M., and Lewicki, R. (eds.). *Negotiating in Organizations*. Thousand Oaks, Calif.: Sage, 1983.

Becker, C., Chasin, L., Chasin, R., Herzig, M., and Roth, S. "From Stuck Debate to New Conversation on Controversial Issues: A Report from the Public Conversations Project." *Journal of Feminist Family Therapy: An International Forum*, 1995, pp. 143–163.

Benne, K., Bradford, L., Gibb, J., and Lippitt, R. (eds.). *The Laboratory Method of Changing and Learning*. Palo Alto, Calif.: Science and Behavior Books, 1975.

Bion, W. *Experiences in Groups, and Other Papers*. New York: Basic Books, 1961.

Blake, R., Shepard, H., and Mouton, J. *Managing Intergroup Conflict in Industry*. Houston: Gulf, 1964.

Bohm, D. *Wholeness and Implicate Order*. London: Routledge, 1980.

Boulding, K. *Conflict and Defense*. New York: HarperCollins, 1962.

Boulding, K. *Three Faces of Power*. Thousand Oaks, Calif.: Sage, 1989.

Brown, L. *Managing Conflict at Organizational Interfaces*. Reading, Mass.: Addison-Wesley, 1983.

Bruner, J. "Life as Narrative." *Social Research*, 1987, *54*(1).

Buber, M. *The Way of Man According to Hasidism*. Secaucus, N.J.: Citadel Press, 1966. (Originally published 1950.)

Buber, M. *I and Thou*. New York: Scribner, 1970. (Originally published 1937.)

Burton, J. W. *Deviance, Terrorism and War*. Suffolk: Martin Robertson, 1979.

Burton, J. W. (ed.). *Conflict: Human Needs Theory*. New York: St. Martin's Press, 1990a.

Burton, J. W. *Conflict: Resolution and Provention*. New York: St. Martin's Press, 1990b.

Carbonneau, T. *Alternative Dispute Resolution: Melting the Lances and Dismounting the Steeds*. Chicago: University of Chicago Press, 1989.

Charme, S. *Meaning and Myth in the Study of Lives: A Sartrean Perspective*. Philadelphia: University of Pennsylvania Press, 1984.

Cohen, S., and Arnone, H. "Conflict Resolution as the Alternative to Terrorism." *Journal of Social Issues*, 1988, *44*(2), 175–190.

Connor, W. *Enthnonationalism: The Quest for Understanding*. Princeton: Princeton University Press, 1994.

Deaux, K. "Personalizing Identity and Socializing Self." In G. Breakwell (ed.), *Social Psychology of Identity and the Self-Concept*. London: Academic Press, 1992.

de Callieres, F. *On the Manner of Negotiating with Princes*. South Bend, Ind.: University of Notre Dame Press, 1963.

de Reuck, A. "Conflict Resolution by Problem Solving." In J. W. Burton and F. Dukes (eds.), *Conflict: Readings in Management and Resolution*. New York: St. Martin's Press, 1990.

Derringer, S. "Rethinking Identity in Conflict: From the Self as Monolith to the Story of Self." Honors Thesis, University of Michigan, Department of Sociology, 1991.

Deutsch, K. *The Nerves of Government*. New York: Free Press, 1963.

Deutsch, M. *The Resolution of Conflict*. New Haven: Yale University Press, 1973.

Doyle, M., and Strauss, D. *How to Make Meetings Work*. New York: Berkley, 1976.

Duke, J. *Conflict and Power in Social Life*. Provo, Utah: Brigham Young University Press, 1976.

Erikson, E. *Childhood and Society*. New York: Norton, 1950.

Etzioni, A. "Social Psychological Aspects of International Relations." In G. Lindzey and E. Aronson (eds.), *Handbook of Social Psychology*, Vol. 5. Reading, Mass.: Addison-Wesley, 1968.

Fisher, R. *The Social Psychology of Intergroup and International Conflict Resolution*. New York: Springer-Verlag, 1990.

Fisher, R., and Ury, W. *Getting to Yes: Negotiating Agreement Without Giving In*. Boston: Houghton Mifflin, 1981.

Folger, J., and Bush, R. *The Promise of Mediation: Responding to Conflict Through Empowerment and Recognition*. San Francisco: Jossey-Bass, 1995.

Follet, M. P. In H. Metcalf and L. Urwick, (eds.), *Dynamic Administration: The Collected Papers of Mary Parker Follet*. New York: HarperCollins, 1941.

Freud, S. *Group Psychology and the Analysis of the Ego*. Standard Edition, *18*, 65–143. London: Hogarth, 1955. (Originally published 1921.)

Galtung, J. "International Development in Human Perspective." In J. W. Burton (ed.), *Conflict: Human Needs Theory*. New York: St. Martin's Press, 1990.

Goffman, E. *Presentation of Self in Everyday Life*. Garden City, N.Y.: Doubleday, 1950.

Goldberg, S., Green, E., and Sander, F. *Dispute Resolution*. Boston: Little, Brown, 1985.

Gross-Stein, J. (ed.). *Getting to the Table: The Processes of International Negotiation*. Baltimore: Johns Hopkins University Press, 1989.

Gurr, T. *Why Men Rebel*. Princeton, N.J: Princeton University Press, 1970.

Habermas, J. *Communication and the Evolution of Society*. Boston: Beacon Press, 1979.

Hare, P. "Pre-Negotiation." *Al Fajr*, May 15, 1989.

Hocker, J., and Wilmot, W. (eds.). *Interpersonal Conflict* (4th ed.). Dubuque, Iowa: William Brown, 1995.

Hogg, M., and Abrams, D. *Social Identifications*. London and New York: Routledge, 1988.

Isaacs, W. "Taking Flight: Dialogue, Collective Thinking, and Organizational Learning." *Organizational Dynamics*, 1993, *22*(2), 24–39.

James, W. *The Moral Equivalent of War*. No. 27. New York: American Association for International Conciliation, 1910.

Jones, E., Kaneouse, D., Kelly, H., Nisbett, R., Valins, S., and Werner, B. (eds.). *Attribution: Perceiving the Causes of Behavior*. Morristown, N.Y.: General Learning Press, 1972.

Jones, M. *Creating the Imaginative Life*. Berkeley, Calif.: Conari Press, 1996.

Jung, C. *The Development of Personality*. New York: Pantheon, 1953.

Kahn, R., and Zald, M. (eds.). *Organizations and Nation-States: New Perspectives on Conflict and Cooperation*. San Francisco: Jossey-Bass, 1990.

Kallen, H. *Cultural Pluralism and the American Idea: An Essay in Social Philosophy*. Philadelphia: University of Pennsylvania Press, 1956.

Katz, D., and Kahn, R. *The Social Psychology of Organizations*. New York: Wiley, 1966.

Kelman, H. "Creating Conditions for Israeli-Palestinian Negotiations." *Journal of Conflict Resolution*, 1982, *26*, 39–75.

Kelman, H. "Coalitions Across Conflict Lines: The Interplay of Conflicts Within and Between the Israeli and Palestinian Communities." In S. Worchel and J. Simpson (eds.), *Conflict Between People and Groups*. Chicago: Nelson-Hall, 1993.

King, M. L., Jr. *Where Do We Go from Here: Chaos or Community?* New York: HarperCollins, 1967.

Kissinger, H. *The Necessity of Choice*. New York: HarperCollins, 1961.

Kottler, J. *Beyond Blame: A New Way of Resolving Conflicts in Relationships*. San Francisco: Jossey-Bass, 1994.

Kriesberg, L., Northrup, T., and Thorson, S. (eds.). *Intractable Conflicts and Their Transformation*. Syracuse, N.Y.: Syracuse University Press, 1989.

Kriesberg, L., and Thorson, S. *Timing the De-escalation of International Conflicts*. Syracuse, N.Y.: Syracuse University Press, 1991.

Lax, D., and Sabenius, J. *The Manager as Negotiator: Bargaining for Cooperation and Competitive Gains*. New York: Free Press, 1986.

Lederach, J. P. *Preparing for Peace: Conflict Transformation Across Cultures*. Syracuse, N.Y.: Syracuse University Press, 1995.

Lewicki, R., and Litterer, J. *Negotiation*. Homewood, Ill.: Irwin, 1985.

Lewin, K. *Resolving Social Conflicts*. New York: HarperCollins, 1948.

Likert, R., and Likert, J. *New Ways of Managing Conflicts*. New York: McGraw-Hill, 1976.

Maslow, A. "A Theory of Motivation." *Psychological Review*, 1943, *50*, 370–396.

Maslow, B. (ed.). *Abraham Maslow: A Memorial Volume*. Pacific Grove, Calif.: Brooks/Cole, 1972, p. 86.

Mayer, R. *Conflict Management: The Courage to Confront*. Columbus, Ohio: Battelle Memorial Institute, 1995.

McGregor, D. *The Human Side of Enterprise*. New York: McGraw-Hill, 1960.

Mehan, H., and Wood, H. *The Reality of Ethnomethodology*. New York: Wiley, 1975.

Mitchell, C., and Banks, M. *Handbook of Conflict Resolution: The Analytical Problem Solving Approach*. London: Pinter, 1996.

Moore, C. W. *The Mediation Process: Practical Strategies for Resolving Conflict*. San Francisco: Jossey-Bass, 1986.

Morgan, G., and Ramirez, R. "Action Learning: A Holographic Metaphor for Guiding Social Change." *Human Relations*, 1984, 37(1), 1–27.

Morgenthau, H. *Politics Among Nations: The Struggle for Power and Peace*. New York: Knopf, 1948.

Northrup, T. "Dynamic of Identity in Personal and Social Conflict." In L. Kriesberg, T. Northrup, and S. Thorson (eds.), *Intractable Conflicts and Their Transformation*. Syracuse, N.Y.: Syracuse University Press, 1989.

Osgood, C. *An Alternative to War or Surrender*. Urbana, Ill.: University of Illinois Press, 1962.

Polyani, M. *The Tacit Dimension*. London: Routledge, 1966.

Pruitt, D., and Rubin, J. *Social Conflict: Escalation, Settlement and Stalemate*. New York: Random House, 1986.

Rafael, G. "Scuttle Diplomacy: The No-Peace Initiative." *Jerusalem Post*, Mar. 30, 1990, p. 4.

Raifa, H. *The Art and Science of Negotiation*. Cambridge, Mass.: Harvard University Press, 1982.

Ross, M. *The Culture of Conflict: Interpretations and Interests in Comparative Perspective*. New Haven: Yale University Press, 1993a.

Ross, M., and Rothman, J. *Theory and Practice in Ethnic Conflict Resolution: Conceptualizing Success and Failure*. London: Macmillan, forthcoming.

Rothman, J. "Negotiation as Consolidation: Prenegotiation in the Israeli-Palestinian Conflict." *Jerusalem Journal of International Relations*, 1991, 13(1), 22–44.

Rothman, J. *From Confrontation to Cooperation: Resolving Ethnic and Regional Conflict*, Thousand Oaks, Calif.: Sage, 1992.

Rothman, J., Land, R., and Twite, R. *The Jerusalem Peace Initiative*. Jerusalem: The Leonard Davis Institute for International Relations, 1994.

Rouhana, N. *Identities in Conflict: Palestinian Citizens in an Ethnic Jewish State*. New Haven: Yale University Press, 1997.

Rouhana, N., and Fiske, S. "Perception of Power, Threat and Conflict Intensity in Asymmetric Intergroup Conflict." *Journal of Conflict Resolution*, 1995, 39, 157–178.

Rousseau, J. J. *The Social Contract*. New York: Putnam, 1893.

Rubin, J., and Brown, B. *The Social Psychology of Bargaining and Negotiation*. New York: Academic Press, 1975.

Rupesinghe, K. *Conflict Transformation*. New York: St. Martin's Press, 1995.

Sarbin, T. *Narrative Psychology: The Storied Nature of Human Conduct*. New York: Praeger, 1986.

Schein, E., and Bennis, W. *Personal and Organizational Change Through Group Methods: The Laboratory Approach*. New York: Wiley, 1965.

Schön, D. *The Reflective Practitioner*. New York: Basic Books, 1983.

Schön, D., and Rein, M. *Frame Reflection*. New York: Basic Books, 1994.

Senge, P. *The Art and Practice of The Learning Organization*. New York: Doubleday, 1990.

Sherif, M., and others. *The Robbers Cave Experiment: Intergroup Conflict and Cooperation*. Middletown, Conn.: Wesleyan University Press, 1988. (Originally published 1961.)

Sherwood, J., and Glidewell, J. "A Planned Renegotiation: A Norm Setting OD Intervention." *Annual Handbook for Group Facilitators*. Iowa City: University Associates Press, 1983.

Sillars, A. "Attributions and Interpersonal Conflict Resolution." In J. Harvey, W. Ickes, and R. Kidd (eds.), *New Directions in Attribution Research* (Vol. 3). Hillsdale, N.J.: Erlbaum, 1981.

Sites, P. *Control, the Basis of Social Order*. New York: Associated Faculty Press, 1973.

Smith, A. "Conflict and Collective Identity: Class, *Ethnie* and Nation." In E. Azar and J. Burton (eds.), *International Conflict Resolution: Theory and Practice*. Sussex: Wheatsheaf, 1986.

Smith, A. *National Identity*. Reno: University of Nevada Press, 1991.

Soros, G. *The Alchemy of Finance*. New York: Wiley, 1987.

Stagner, R., and Rosen, H. *Psychology of Union-Management Relations*. Pacific Grove, Calif.: Brooks/Cole, 1965.

Steir, F. (ed.). *Reflexivity and Research*. Thousand Oaks, Calif.: Sage, 1991.

Susskind, L., and Cruikshank, J. *Breaking the Impasse: Consensual Approaches to Resolving Public Disputes*. New York: Basic Books, 1987.

Tajfel, H. *Human Groups and Social Categories: Studies in Social Psychology*. Cambridge: Cambridge University Press, 1981.

Taylor, F. *The Principles of Scientific Management*. New York: HarperCollins, 1911.

Thomas, K. "Conflict and Conflict Management." In M. Dunnette (ed.), *Handbook of Industrial and Organizational Psychology*. Chicago: Rand McNally, 1976.

Tjosvold, D. *The Conflict Positive Organization: Stimulate Diversity and Create Unity*. New York: Addison-Wesley, 1992.

Traub, J. "Onward and Upward with the Arts: Passing the Baton, Workplace Democracy in the Orpheus Chamber Orchestra." *The New Yorker,* Aug/Sept 1996, pp. 100–105.

Ury, W. *Getting Past No: Negotiating with Difficult People.* New York: Bantam, 1991.

Volkan, V. *The Need to Have Enemies and Allies: From Clinical Practice to International Relationships.* Northvale, N.J.: Aronson, 1988.

Walton, R., and McKersie, R. *A Behavioral Theory of Labor Negotiations: An Analysis of a Social System.* New York: McGraw-Hill, 1965.

Walton, R., and McKersie, R. "Behavioral Dilemmas in Mixed-Motive Decision Making." *Behavioral Science,* 1966, *11,* 370–384.

Watzlawicki, P., Wakland, J., and Fisch, R. *Change: Principles of Problem Formulation and Problem Resolution.* New York: Norton, 1974.

Weber, M. *The Theory of Social and Economic Organization.* New York: Free Press, 1947.

White, R. *Fearful Warriors: A Psychological Profile of U.S. Soviet Relations.* New York: Free Press, 1984.

Woosley, R. "The Fifth Column: La Methode de Charles Maurice de Talleyrand or Maximized Acceptance with Optimized Agendas." *Interfaces,* Nov/Dec 1991, *21,* 103–105.

Zartman, W., and Berman, M. *The Practical Negotiator.* New Haven, Conn.: Yale University Press, 1982.

Index

CPSIA information can be obtained at www.ICGtesting.com
Printed in the USA
BVOW08*0802270316

441216BV00020B/40/P

9 780787 909963